The Development of
Conversation and *Discourse*

edited by

TERRY MYERS

at the **Edinburgh** *University Press*

© Edinburgh University Press 1979
22 George Square, Edinburgh

ISBN 0 85224 360 X

Printed in Great Britain by
Brown, Knight & Truscott Ltd
Tonbridge, Kent

PREFACE

The idea of putting forward a book on *The Development of Conversation and Discourse* came from a small symposium, with that title, organised within the Department of Psychology at Edinburgh University in May, 1975. Though the subject was not new, it had not received much treatment during the preceding fifteen years or so of developmental psycholinguistics. And despite short notice of the symposium, a large audience gathered both from within the University and from neighbouring institutions. The time was clearly right for re-opening scientific discussion of this complex subject. So encouraged, the participants agreed to make those adjustments to their papers necessary to ensure their coherence within a single volume whilst preserving the spontaneity of the original presentations. When the main body of the book had been completed, it was sent to Ken Reeder, who agreed to write a concluding chapter by way of a critical comment. An introductory chapter was then prepared by the editor. A version of that chapter was submitted to the Working Group on Speech Acts at the XIIth International Congress of Linguistics, Vienna 1977.

Margaret Bullowa opened the symposium by proposing that the infant has some capacity for communication at birth and soon engages in communicative exchanges with his caretaker about the *I-thou* relationship. With the subsequent development of *deixis* a third term is introduced into the relationship, one that enables an exchange to be about either a third person, an object, or an event. Margaret, who died on 18 May 1978, is remembered in Edinburgh with affection.

Henry Widdowson addressed himself to the relationship between the *rules* comprising the interlocutor's competence and the *procedures* that characterise his performance. He proposed two types of rules: *rules of usage*, which constitute the grammatical source of reference, and *rules of use*, which constitute the communicative source of reference. Corresponding to these are two types of procedures whereby a discourse may have propositional cohesion and illocutionary coherence: *cohesion procedures* and *coherence procedures*. And whereas the two types of rules are related by *modality*, the two types of procedures are linked by *interactivity*.

Michael Halliday described the development of conversation from *acts of communication* early after birth to the later, pre-verbal *acts of meaning*. As the child moves into the mother tongue, acts of meaning begin to have the property referred to as *texture*. The three main aspects of textual meanings are: i) the internal texture of the clause, in terms of information and thematic structure, ii) the external cohesive relations of reference, substitution and conjunction, and iii) the generic properties of narrative and dialogue.

John Lyons discussed the development of *reference*, showing how *anaphora* builds ontogenetically on deixis, and suggested *textual deixis* as an intermediate stage in this process. Language he argued, provides the means for reference to entities in the *universe-of-discourse,* upon which anaphora crucially depends.

Ken Reeder examined the work presented by the contributors to the symposium in the context of recent research in child discourse and drew some implications for the educational field.

In my introduction I explore, within the descriptive framework of Speech Act Theory, the relationship between the verbal and the non-verbal *interactive acts* that comprise conversation. The non-verbal acts may be sub-classified into three main types: *iso-verbal, indexical* and *meta-communicative*. The part played by the first two of these in the developmental shift to verbal interactivity is also considered.

Terry Myers, Edinburgh, January 1979.

CONTENTS

VERBAL AND NON-VERBAL INTERACTIVITY

Introduction

Psycholinguistic theory had not, until quite recently, seemed a very rich source of questions about the development of conversation and discourse. Although the vigorous sixties and early seventies saw a rapid growth of interest mainly in the child's acquisition of the structural rules of his native language, but also in the relationship between the resulting structures and those of his developing cognitive system, little attention was directed at the child's developing use of language for the purposes of social interaction. More recently, however, some developmental psycholinguists have helped to redress this comparative neglect, the new direction of their work being encouraged perhaps, by two important shifts in theoretical perspective: one from the structure of language to its functions, the other from the child as a thinking individual to the child as a communicator. That they have been able to orientate in this way is largely attributable to work on *illocutionary acts* by philosophers of language (e.g., Austin 1962, and Searle 1969). In this paper an attempt will be made to apply some of the concepts arising from that work to the investigation of two major questions underlying research on conversation and its development. They concern: i) the co-ordination of verbal and non-verbal interactive acts in conversation and ii) the developmental shift from pre-verbal to verbal interactivity. The discussion will turn mainly around the first of these questions. We will touch only lightly on the second (see concluding section) in order just to indicate an approach. It is taken up again by some of the other contributors to the symposium (Bullowa, Halliday, Lyons).

Discourse and Conversation

Discourse may be defined as any form of verbal interactivity, whether spoken or written (Widdowson, pers.comm). Such a broad definition embraces both i) instances in which the interactivity is not realised as behaviour on the part of the addressee(s), whose influence on the discourse derives from what the speaker (or writer) anticipates *would be* his reactions (cf. a spoken address, and a letter), and ii) instances in which the interactivity *is* realised by reciprocal behaviour between addressor and addressee, in which case the discourse satisfies the minimal conditions for describing it as a conversation. However, the interactivity of conversation, as we shall see, is realised by both verbal and non-verbal behaviour, and our definition needs to be tailored accordingly: conversation is verbal and non-verbal interactivity realised by reciprocal behaviour between at least two people, who alternate in the roles of addressor and addressee. 'Talking-to-oneself' would count as conversation if we allow that 'addressor' and 'addressee' are roles that may be played by an externalised self or an internalised other. An infant on the other hand, who by definition is pre-verbal, may not accordingly be said to engage in conversation. However, to the extent that he may be capable of non-verbal interactivity, we shall say that he *is* able to engage in *proto-conversation* (cf. De Laguna 1927, and Bullowa, this Symposium).

Conversational Interactivity

Prompted by our definition of conversation, we will propose two main types of *interactive act* in conversation, the verbal and the non-verbal. We will examine each of these in turn and in some detail, before taking up the questions raised in our introductory remarks.

Verbal Interactive Acts

A verbal interactive act in conversational discourse is what we take to be an illocutionary act. Three major classes of illocutionary act are *statement, question* and *mand* (see Lyons 1977: vol. 2, for the use of the term 'mand'. 'Request' and 'command' are members of this class). Although the theoretical status of the illocutionary act is still being negotiated among linguists, psycholinguists and philosophers of language, there is growing acceptance of it as the unit of linguistic communication. There is less agreement concerning the assignment of structural descriptions to illocutionary acts. In their *literal* performance, statements, questions and mands are realised grammatically by the sentence types *declarative, interrogative* and *jussive* respectively (see Lyons, op. cit.). In the literal performance of a mand a speaker produces a sentence of the jussive type, for example, 'Give me a light!'. A theoretical problem arises when the illocutionary act is performed non-literally, as in the case of a mand being realised by an interrogative sentence: 'Can you give me a light?'. In this example the *indirect* illocutionary act is a mand that is softened to a request, a polite form of the mand, by the choice of an interrogative sentence type. The verbal act in this case conveys the *illocutionary force* of a request.

What is seemingly paradoxical about the indirect illocutionary act is how the addressee knows which illocutionary force was intended, if not the one corresponding directly with the choice of sentence type. To resolve this paradox we must shift our theoretical focus from grammar to pragmatics (cf. Gordon and Lakoff 1971; Searle 1975; Sinclair and Coulthard 1975, and Miller and Johnson-Laird 1976). For example, Searle's account of indirect illocutionary acts includes: certain non-linguistic[1] conditions on the 'felicitous' performance of an illocutionary act; 'general principles of co-operative conversation' (cf. Grice 1975); the ability of the addressee to make inferences, and the sharing of background factual information between addressor and addressee. It is the sharing of background information that ensures that 'Can you give me the moon?' will be taken as a literal, if allegorical and even rhetorical question, rather than an indirect request, as was the case with 'Can you give me a light?'.

Although this is not the place to evaluate Searle's solution of the problem of indirect illocutionary acts against the possibility of generative-semantic alternatives (cf. Ross 1970; Jackendoff 1972, and Sadock 1972 and 1975), we may note that his exclusion of 'conversational postulates' from his account is a point of disagreement with Gordon and Lakoff.

On the other hand, Sinclair and Coulthard's classification of illocutionary acts by *situation*, which includes 'relevant factors in the environment, social conventions, and shared experience of the participants' is nearly coincident with the account given by Searle if we take his role of inference to be implicit, at least, in the system of Sinclair and Coulthard.

An important, if indirect, outcome of the pragmatic approach to illocutionary acts is that it suggests a way of inferring the addressor's *communicative intention* (see p.26 and note 16) in the case not only of a verbal interactive act, but of a non-verbal interactive act as well. A pragmatic account of communicative intention, together with a principle we will refer to as *functional equivalence*[2] (see p.7), will enable us to take a few steps towards the solution of the questions concerning the co-ordination of verbal and non-verbal interactive acts, and the developmental shift from pre-verbal to verbal interactive acts. Before we can take those steps, however, we have some more conceptual ground to prepare.

Our discussion of illocutionary acts has been directed at the communicative intentions conveyed in their performance. We will need also, for our understanding of the development of conversation, to consider the *propositional content* of the illocutionary act. Discussions of the proposition usually draw a distinction between a *referential component* that, in the simplest case, enables identification of an object or event in the physical world, that is, *first-order* and *second-order entities* respectively, in Lyons' account (this Symposium), and a *predicative component*, whereby something may be said about the entity referred to. In adult conversation of course, the referent will not always be either a first-order or a second-order entity (cf. 'Kindness is a virtue'), and a number of extensions to the concept of reference are necessary. For the discussion of the earliest stages of conversation on the other hand, such extensions are not likely to be required. We will require though, some agreement concerning the way that propositional content and illocutionary force may be said to be related, in both the 'literal' and the 'indirect' cases.

Searle (1969) pointed out that in the performance of different illocutionary acts the propositional content may remain the same, for example, 'You are leaving (I see)', 'Are you leaving?' and 'Leave!' all predicate 'leave' of 'you' ('you leave'). The propositional content is neutral with respect to the illocutionary force. This observation entails the important consequence for theory that in the analysis of illocutionary acts, propositional content and illocutionary force may be treated separately. Indeed Widdowson (1973 and this Symposium) has explored the implications of this separability in his discussion of the organisation of discourse. However, though separable for the purposes of theoretical analysis, illocutionary force and propositional content are not mutually independent in behaviour. Thus, whilst an illocutionary act need not have any propositional content (Searle's examples are 'Hurrah!' and 'Ouch!'), a proposition may not be expressed except in the performance of an illocutionary act.

An interesting problem arises when we examine the question of how illocutionary force and propositional content are conveyed in the case of *ellipsis*, which is very common in both child and adult conversation. When fully expressed, the illocutionary force may be realised by such devices as mood and tense of the verb; word order; punctuation (written discourse) and intonation (spoken discourse). But often, neither the illocutionary force nor the propositional content are fully realised in the surface structure of an utterance. Consider the utterance of a surgeon to his assistant during an operation: 'Forceps?', an uncommonly polite way to perform a mand perhaps, in this context. Ross (1970) and others since have argued that in the case of ellipsis, illocutionary force as well as propositional content, is represented in sentence form at a deep structure level. Whether or not that may be the case for the addressor, we will assume that for the addressee, at least, the only linguistic correlate of illocutionary force in our example, is the intonation contour of its spoken realisation. Accordingly, it would seem to be a matter of pragmatics that the act realised in the use of the question intonation is to be interpreted in this case as an indirect request. In other words, the relation of intonation to illocutionary force, like that of illocutionary force to grammatical means of expression, is complex. It may, on the other hand, prove to be the case, as Sag and Liberman's (1975) data suggest, that intonation is systematically employed as a means to contrast the literal and the indirect force of an illocutionary act. Thus the force of a mand in our example may be conveyed directly by a *sharp* rise in contour. That is, intonation may be more closely related than surface syntax to a speaker's communicative intention, as Myers (1975) suggested, but we will not pursue that suggestion on this occasion.

Returning to our discussion of propositional content, we will suppose that in performing propositional acts, the addressor expresses verbally those *mental operations* corresponding to the causal structure of events, states and relations associated with objects and persons. In company with Bates (1976), we will consider such mental operations to comprise the meaning or content of a given proposition, and assume, though it would be difficult to verify, that the addressor intends the same mental operations to take place in the addressee. He intends in other words, by his performance of some propositional act, that the addressee will form a mental representation of the relations predicated of the entities identified by the corresponding acts of reference. And it is his communicative intention that in performing the illocutionary act the addressee will recognise the illocutionary force with which the corresponding propositional act is performed. Considering the example involving the proposition 'you leave', the addressee must be able to perform the corresponding mental representation, that of the entity referred to, himself, performing the act of leaving, and also recognise that the addressor is either stating it as the case, enquiring whether it is the case, or demanding that it be so. Much of this as we have indicated, may be achieved by pragmatic means. However, to the extent that the illocutionary act is grammatically realised, the illocutionary force will be expressed in terms of the *mood component* (cf. Halliday 1973, and Lyons 1977: vol. 2), and the propositional content in terms of the *transitivity component* (cf. Halliday 1973, and Lyons 1968) of the language being used. In learning to use the mood component of a language the child acquires the means to express his communicative intention concerning the entities and relationships in a given proposition, and in learning to use the transitivity component he is enabled to express his knowledge or perception of such entities and relationships, and thereby to give propositional content to his illocutionary act. The third major component in Halliday's system (cf. Halliday 1973 and 1975), the *textual component*, is the one that will enable the child to employ the other two for the purpose of engaging in conversation.

Without going well beyond the scope of this introduction, we cannot explore in any detail how propositional content and communicative intention are brought together in the performance of a verbal interactive act, either in terms of psychological operations or of grammatical organisation. But some consideration of this problem would be necessary in order to formulate a complete answer to each of our main questions concerning the co-ordination of non-verbal and verbal interactive acts and the developmental shift from pre-verbal to verbal interactive acts. In order to make a start, a first requirement will be that of providing a description of non-verbal interactive acts.

Non-Verbal Interactive Acts
Non-verbal interactivity has been the subject of intense study recently by ethnomethodologists, ethologists and sociolinguists. We will restrict our observations to those non-verbal interactive acts that occur when people engage in informal, face-to-face conversation. Abercrombie (1968) takes such acts (whether vocal or non-vocal) to be instances of paralinguistic behaviour. Our category of non-verbal behaviour will be expanded to include intonation, which is linguistic (Lyons 1972). We will sub-divide this behaviour into three types of act: *iso-verbal, indexical* and *meta-communicative*. Our classification is intended to be neutral with regard to the behavioural medium of expression: vocalisation, gesture, facial expression, eye-contact, proximity, posture and orientation (but see Key 1970).[3] But it is motivated by considerations of function, as we shall see later.

Iso-verbal acts are *functionally equivalent* to verbal acts which they may replace in conversational discourse. That is, an iso-verbal act may realise or indicate the whole or part of an illocutionary act that could otherwise be fully realised verbally. Clear examples of iso-verbal acts are a nod and a shake of the head in place of 'yes' and 'no' respectively; the sound 'shh' for 'Be quiet!'; a gesture of pressing the forefinger flat against the lips for 'Don't say anything!', and certain gestures (e.g., a sinuous movement with the hands to represent the female form) which are termed 'emblems' by Ekman and Friesen (1969). Such acts, we are proposing, may realise the whole or part of an illocutionary act.

Lyons (1977) points out that the theory of illocutionary acts does not rule out the possibility of the illocution being realised non-verbally, and Bates (1976) defines it as the 'intentional use of a conventional signal to carry out some socially recognised function', where 'a conventional signal' may be either verbal or non-verbal. We will take as part of our definition of an iso-verbal act, that its product in one or more of the media of expression is a conventional signal. But interpretation of the illocution realised in the performance of an iso-verbal act is not always as straightforward as in the clear examples just cited. In this respect it will be appropriate to sub-divide iso-verbal acts into three sub-types. The clear examples belong to type I, and bear a fixed relationship with the meanings they are used to express: the propositional content and illocutionary force are fixed by convention. Interpretation of type I iso-verbal acts is independent of context. But this statement needs to be qualified. Consider the case of shaking the head to mean 'no'. By performing a similar movement on some given occasion one may intend simply to dodge an insect that is about to land on one's nose. Another gesture, with the hand, signals the command '(You) stop!', but it could also be used to ward off an unwelcome approach. The behaviours that realise iso-verbal acts, then, may on occasions also occur '*non*-semiotically'. The *context-of-interaction*[4] needs to be taken into account for identifying such occasions. The behaviour that realises a verbal act, on the other hand, does not have a non-semiotic function. In the utterance of 'no' a *locutionary act*[5] is performed whatever the context.

A further qualification regarding the contextual independence of type I iso-verbal acts may be illustrated using the example of the pointing gesture. It is a conventional signal whose basic meanings are fixed independently of context. That is, it may be either an entity-referring or a place-referring act (see Lyons 1975, and this Symposium). Which meaning is intended on a given occasion, however, is determined *in context*. Thus a pointing gesture, immediately followed by a summoning gesture with the same hand, may be glossed as '(You) come here!', where the pointing gesture in this case is clearly entity-referring. It is largely a matter of convention that the second gesture expresses both the predicative component of the proposition 'you come' and the illocutionary force of a 'mand'. These two gestures are of course usually combined into a single gesture, and in some contexts, may be performed simultaneously with an appropriate indexical act (e.g., smile), which softens the mand, turning it into an invitation.

Type II iso-verbal acts may not be so readily characterised, and their theoretical status is no more than that of a working hypothesis to be examined by further observation and experiment. We will therefore hypothesise that there are interactive acts that, though they use conventional *signals*, do not realise illocutionary acts independently of context. In context, however, an act of this type may be used to *indicate* an illocutionary act whose propositional content and/or illocutionary force have to be inferred from the given context. One may express the illocutionary act indicated with such a signal by means of a verbal gloss. Thus a gesture with the hand, palm facing upwards, may be glossed verbally as 'Give it to me!'; 'After you!' or 'Would you like to (try/speak/ . . .)?', and so on, depending upon the context. Although the choice between alternative interpretations may be partially constrained by additional components of the total gesture (e.g., eye contact, facial expression, tilt of the head, position of the arm), the propositional content and illocutionary force of an equivalent verbal act that the gesture may be said to replace, and that we project into a verbal gloss, are to be inferred from the interactional context by *pragmatic procedures*.[6] Such procedures play an important part in the interpretation of elliptical verbal acts and indirect illocutionary acts as we have seen. And so, 'After you!', 'Please!' and a functionally equivalent iso-verbal act may each be interpreted as an invitation to the addressee to take precedence over the addressor, given that the context is 'appropriate'. Of course a 'natural language' furnishes a rich array of lexical and syntactic means by which the propositional content and illocutionary force of a verbal interactive act may be fully expressed independently of interactional context. But informal conversation draws heavily on pragmatic procedures, and it is by means of such procedures, we are suggesting, that an iso-verbal interactive act of this type may indicate the functionally equivalent verbal interactive act that we try to capture in the verbal gloss.

Type III iso-verbal acts are realised as intonation contours. As we indicated earlier, the illocutionary force of a verbal interactive act is realisable not only by means of syntactic devices such as mood of the verb. In the case of speaking, it is also realised by means of intonation contour. That is, intonation contour is an iso-verbal component of the spoken verbal act, one that enables the force of the act to be conveyed even in the absence of syntactic force-indicating devices. But does it do so in a context-independent way?

Now, of course, the role of context for the interpretation of intonation contour has been widely attested in the literature, and we do not wish to gainsay the conclusions reached by others. Gunter (1972), for example, has demonstrated that the contour on a given utterance determines its 'relevance' to the preceding utterance in discourse, and that the relevance associated with a given contour does not transfer to a new context. Thus the relevance of the utterances 'Tea' with a falling contour, will be different following 'What did he drink?' from its relevance following 'John drank wine'. The *relevance* conveyed by a contour is therefore clearly context-dependent. Nevertheless, and in order to provoke further study, we will hypothesise a context-free convention with regard to the relationship between intonation contour (more specifically, 'tone') and *illocutionary force*. In the 'neutral' case at least (see Halliday 1970b), tone 1 (falling) signals that an act is either a statement, a WH-question, or a mand, whilst tone 2 (rising) signals a yes/no question. Moreover, it is on the basis of such a convention arguably, that pragmatic procedures may operate to determine the indirect force corresponding to a given tone in a given context (e.g., 'Forceps?', with tone 2). The way that context may enter into the interpretation of iso-verbal acts of type III puts this type in an intermediate position between types I and II.

Our second class of non-verbal interactive acts, indexical acts, provides information to the addressee about the addressor himself. This use of the term 'index' was introduced by Peirce (1932). One of his earliest examples, as relayed to me by David Abercrombie, is the 'rolling gait' of a sailor on dry land. The walk is an indexical sign of what it is causally attributable to, the rolling deck of a ship at sea. In speech, the audible features of 'voice quality' which are causally attributable to anatomical properties of the articulatory apparatus, are, analogously, indexical signs of an adult speaker's identity, sex and age. Such features, which are instances of Abercrombie's (1967) class of 'idiosyncratic indices', enable recognition of a person by voice alone, and are an inevitable property of vocalisation from birth, though sex-distinguishing features of voice may not be measurably significant in infancy. Other indexical features of the audible and visible behaviour of an infant, which are causally attributable to physical states, are those associated with, for example, hunger and pain. Indices, which are signs of the physical conditions that cause them, correspond to 'indexes' in Piaget's (1970) usage. Piaget used the concept of 'index' in describing the infant's 'cognitive function', stating that indexes 'play a role' in the first few weeks of life. He was referring to the infant as *recipient* of indexical features, whilst we will be concerned with the role of the infant as both recipient and emitter of indexical *acts*. And whereas indices of the causal type (or indexes) will not therefore be relevant for our discussion, we should bear in mind that they very likely play an important role in the formation of 'affectional bonds' between mother and infant. What we would suggest is that a component of the infant's resources for what Malinowski (1923) described as 'phatic communion' and Bullowa (this Symposium) describes as communication about the 'I-thou' relationship comprises indexical acts, and these we will argue later, are *intentional*. There is not to my knowledge any data that directly supports such a suggestion, attempts to investigate it having been inhibited perhaps, by a climate of opinion in which the infant has been regarded as 'ego-centric'. But this viewpoint is now changing (see Reeder's comments on the Symposium).

Indexical acts in our usage are those expressive acts that serve a 'social-emotional' function. They give expression, that is, to the attitudes and feelings that are basic ingredients in the formation and maintenance of inter-personal relationships during conversation and proto-conversation. The property of conversational speech that manifests such states of the speaker has been called 'tone of voice' (Abercrombie 1967). In Abercrombie's terms, it comprises 'affective indices', which are conveyed by, for example, voice-pitch fluctuations ('vocal gestures') that are superimposed on the intonation contour, and 'register differences', which arise from adjustments to the action of phonation. Examples of non-vocal indexical acts are the smile and the frown. But any behavioural means may be employed in the performance of indexical acts, and different cultures vary in the ways that such means are deployed for this purpose. Effective social-emotional communication relies very much upon the acquisition of the indexical resources of one's culture. And although indexical acts may usually be replaced by verbal acts (cf. Searle's 'principle of expressibility'), they frequently have an immediacy that is difficult to match verbally.

Our third class of non-verbal interactive acts is the one we are describing as 'meta-communicative'. Meta-communicative acts serve the general function of regulating the interactional process. Acts of this type may, for example: i) signal a permitted shift in addressor-addressee role (cf. Kendon 1967, 1973; Duncan 1972, 1973); ii) censure deviations from co-operative procedures, such as infringement of 'turn-taking' rules (cf. Scheflen 1972), and iii) segment what Goffman (1974) calls the 'story line' into 'idea units' and 'information units' by means of gesture (cf. Kendon 1976; Butterworth and Beattie 1976) and intonation: for example, 'tonic placement', for marking a distinction between 'given' and 'new' information in the concurrent verbal act (cf. Halliday 1970b),[7] and 'tone unit' boundary (Crystal 1975). A meta-communicative act is one that regulates the performance or the interpretation of an associated interactive act (verbal or non-verbal). Our use of the term 'meta-communicative' has its origin in the work of Gregory Bateson (1955).

Functions of Interactive Acts

At the level of the distinctions we have now drawn in our description of verbal and non-verbal interactive acts, they may be said to serve three major interactive functions in adult conversation: *ideational-informative, F1*, which concerns the exchange of ideas (i.e., products of mental operations), *social-emotional, F2*, which concerns regulation of interpersonal relationships, and *F3, interaction-regulating*, which concerns management of the co-operative process whereby conversational text is generated.

The distinction between F1 and F2, which reflects that of Bühler (1934) between 'representational' and 'conative-expressive' appears to have the approval of a number of linguists. For Abercrombie (1968) the distinction is between 'referential' and 'emotive'; for Lyons (1972) 'cognitive' and 'social'; for Halliday (1970a) 'ideational' and 'interpersonal', and for Crystal (1975) 'cognitive' and 'affective'. Moreover, F2, which is associated with Malinowski's notion of phatic communion, also corresponds to Bateson's (1966) 'μ-function', which 'concerns the rules and contingencies of relationship'. According to Bateson, communication among animals serves primarily μ-functions, and although man has words for these (e.g., 'love' and 'dependency'), such 'digital' means are not seen to be as effective for these purposes as indexical acts. On the other hand, though human language is thought to be specially adapted for F1-type communication, we cannot claim that animal communication does not serve F1 functions. Recent studies with chimpanzees (e.g., Menzel 1971 and 1975) throw doubt on any such claim. Indeed, the differences between man and animals with regard to their resources for communication is arguably to be sought not in terms of 'function' but in terms of 'structure'. Thus, animal communication systems may be 'bi-stratal', having the levels of 'content' and 'expression' only, whilst the linguistic system is 'tri-stratal', with grammar interposed between the other two (cf. Halliday 1975). Which emphasis we take up, structure or function, has important consequences both for our understanding of systems of communication in general, and more especially, for our approach to the two questions we posed in the introduction. Our choice of a functional emphasis with regard to those more specific issues is intended to be neutral with regard to the difficult theoretical question of the relationship between linguistic structure and interactive function. But the functional emphasis will not prevent our consideration of structures where this is appropriate. F3 corresponds to Halliday's 'textual' function.

Clearly our functional distinctions are closely related to those of Halliday, and broadly correspond also to Laver and Hutcheson's (1972) three types of information exchanged during conversation: 'cognitive', 'indexical' and 'interaction-management' (see also Argyle 1972). But whilst our classification of verbal and non-verbal acts was largely motivated by considerations of function, the categories of interactive acts that we obtained do not map into these three functions in a simple, one-to-one fashion. An examination of the differences in this respect between verbal and non-verbal interactive acts will provide a lever on the question of how they are co-ordinated in conversation.

The Co-ordination of Verbal and Non-Verbal Interactive Acts in Conversation

Our approach to the question of the co-ordination of verbal and non-verbal interactive acts rests upon the principle of 'functional equivalence'. We will offer only a preliminary account here and take up the question again elsewhere.

Now, Halliday (1973) took the 'clause' to be 'the simultaneous realisation of ideational, interpersonal and textual meaning', and demonstrated how these meanings are realised in terms of the transitivity, mood (and modality) and textual components, respectively, of grammar. We will consider how the corresponding functions of our system relate first, to the propositional content and illocutionary force of the verbal interactive act, and second, to our three types of non-verbal interactive act.

Propositional acts serve primarily an ideational-informative function, but not exclusively, for the lexical selections associated with the referential and predicative components of a proposition may, at the same time, reflect both the interaction-regulating and the social-emotional functions as well. Consider the sentence: 'The shop-steward challenged/invited him to answer'. Choice of the 'anaphoric' element 'him', which indicates co-referentiality with a lexical item employed in a previous verbal act, rests upon shared assumptions and rules for co-operative conversation and text construction, and these are an interaction-regulating matter. Choice between 'challenged' and 'invited', moreover, is a social-emotional matter, being sensitive to the relative 'social status' and 'role' of each of the persons referred to as 'the shop-steward' and 'him'. The verbs in this example do not, however, make explicit the emotion that may have been displayed by the shop-steward. Other verbs do: for example, 'He frowned/ smiled his disapproval/approval', in which an indexical act (a frown or a smile, each of which may be genuine or affected) is referred to directly. The difference between the verbs selected in our two examples corresponds to the [± Linguistic] feature distinction employed in the analysis of verbs by Ross (1970). The distinction might for our purposes be better described by the feature [± Indexical]. It would seem then that, although the propositional act serves primarily the ideational-informative function, the lexical realisation of its referential and predicative components may at the same time serve the social-emotional and interaction-regulating functions.

We saw earlier that the illocutionary force of a verbal interactive act may be adapted (e.g., softened) to perform a social-emotional function, but more generally the illocutionary force of a verbal interactive act corresponds to the addressor's communicative intention with regard to the propositional act. And to the extent that the addressee responds in terms of his comprehension of that intention, so illocutionary force serves to regulate the interactional process: it has an interaction-regulating function. Indeed it is commonly understood as a rule of co-operative conversation that when, for example, one is asked a question an answer is called for. The question-and-answer is a major type of 'adjacency pair' (Schegloff and Sacks 1973), and the performance of an 'adjacency pair first part' is one device for cueing the addressee to take a 'turn' by responding with the second part (Sacks, Schegloff and Jefferson 1974). But the effect of illocutionary force on the operation of the turn-taking system is not direct. To illustrate this point let us examine further the question-and-answer example.

On some occasion of use, a question may not be *intended* to call for an answer. It may be only one of a sequence of illocutionary acts within a single turn, and not necessarily the one to which the addressee will be expected to respond. The question may, for example, have been used rhetorically or simply as an attention-focussing device. Knowing when a question calls for an answer requires the participants in the conversation to operate at a level of *discourse* functioning, one Sinclair and Coulthard refer to as the *move*. We may, continuing with their terminology, think of the adjacency pair as comprising a first move, which serves an *initiating* function in the discourse, and a second, which serves a *response* function. Initiating and response moves are themselves con-structed from units that Sinclair and Coulthard describe as *discourse acts*, and one type of discourse act that occurs as the head of an initiating move is the *elicitation*. [8] Now it is only on those occasions when a question is realising an elicitation that it will call for an answer, which is an appropriate realisation of a *reply*. That is, the co-operative response to an elicitation is a reply, which is one of the types of discourse act used to realise a response move. The question-and-answer, in other words, is the illocutionary realisation of that type of adjacency pair, which at the level of discourse acts is an 'elicitation-and-reply', and at the level of moves is an 'initiation-and-response'.

It would appear then that the relationship between illo-cutionary force and turn-taking behaviour in conversation must be accounted for in terms of the participants' knowledge of the rules associated with the sequencing of discourse acts, rules comprising what Sinclair and Coulthard refer to as *tactics*. Although we are not in a position yet to formulate these rules with any degree of generality, or to say how they relate to corresponding *procedures* for performing a sequence of discourse acts (see Widdowson, this Symposium), we will nevertheless assume their existence. Indeed, the ability of subjects partially to reconstruct discourse sequences from utterance-length excerpts, has been largely attributed to the existence of such rules (cf. Abramovici and Myers 1975, and Clarke 1975).

The data of Sinclair and Coulthard included a number of discourse acts that were non-verbal, particularly when they realised a response move. Now this is arguably a local feature of teacher-pupil discourse of a certain type, in which the instructional style of the teacher appears to have closely constrained the pupils to respond not only with rather short verbal responses, but with non-verbal ones as well, most of which were actions in response to a directive. Indeed, the resulting texts are reminiscent of the kind reported by Labov (1969), following an interview with an apparently 'mono-syllabic' child. The child's fluency was demonstrably increased, however, when the interviewer adopted certain strategies for reducing the status difference between himself and the child. On the other hand, video recordings of husband-and-wife conversations (Shepherd 1976) confirmed our intuition that the occasional non-verbal realisation of discourse acts is a normal feature of informal conversation between people who know each other well. What is more, when we extend our observation to include indexical acts and iso-verbal acts, type III, we immediately find that non-verbal interactive acts are an important and ubiquitous feature of conversation. Rather than 'discourse act' therefore we will use the term *conversational act*, which by definition may be verbal or non-verbal. We are now faced with the question: how are verbal and non-verbal interactive acts co-ordinated in conversation? We will examine this question concurrently with our consideration of the functions of non-verbal acts, beginning with the iso-verbal type.

Verbal and Iso-Verbal Acts
During our discussion of iso-verbal acts we introduced the concept of functional equivalence, equivalence, that is, in the sense that an iso-verbal act may realise, or at least 'indicate', the same illocutionary act, or a component of it, as the verbal act it is said to replace in the discourse. In structural terms, of course, an iso-verbal act and its verbal correlate are quite different, and a moment's consideration of some of the differences, at this point, may be helpful in our attempt to

understand the way in which verbal and iso-verbal acts are co-ordinated in conversation.

Whereas verbal acts are composed of elements that are re-combinable with others to form a large, open class of illocutionary acts, iso-verbal acts are not decomposable in this way and form by comparison a small, finite set. They display the 'bi-stratal' property by which Halliday (1975) characterised the 'proto-language' of the child. Type I comprises a small set of content-expression pairs. Type II would seem also to comprise a relatively small set, but they may in principle, at least, be mapped into a large number of meanings, as determined by the different contexts into which they enter. Type III (tones) are by consensus a small, closed set, although linguists do not agree about the number in the set. And so, for example, the number of main types are, according to Halliday: 5 (primary tones), and Crystal: 7+. The different numbers arise from the alternative approaches to the problem of determining the linguistic function of tone. Halliday's (1970b) approach is in terms of a relationship between tone and the major speech functions, and these correspond to our three major categories of illocutionary force, except for the further distinction between yes/no-and WH-questions. Crystal (1975), on the other hand, argues that our choice of the set of distinctions should be determined according to which of them 'can be shown to expound categories already required by a grammar', and provides examples for six such grammatical distinctions. Since, however, further consideration of these distinctions would take us beyond the scope of this discussion, we will for current purposes at least, continue from the position we have already adopted, namely, that the linguistic function of tone is primarily that of 'expounding' those major categories of illocutionary force that correspond to the major sentence types.

Taking up the question of the co-ordination of interactive acts in conversation we will first examine the use of constructions resulting from the combination of sentences and then look at the constraints on the simultaneous performance of a verbal and an iso-verbal act.

There appear to be two ways in which sentences may be combined in the performance of verbal acts: by 'embedding' and by 'conjoining' (cf. Chomsky 1957 and Lyons 1968). Thus: 'Jimmy Carter once grew peanuts' and 'Jimmy Carter is now the President' may be combined to form the embedded construction: 'Jimmy Carter who once grew peanuts is now the President', or the conjoined construction: 'Jimmy Carter once grew peanuts and he is now the President'. The embedded and the conjoined constructions each preserve the propositional content of the original two sentences. But now, what is the illocutionary force of the act performed in the use of one of these constructions?

Consider the case of embedding: the illocutionary force of an act employing such a construction may be associated, we suggest, with the clause that is directly dominated by the top-most S-node of its underlying phrase-marker. The force would accordingly be that associated with the main clause. To test this we require to examine instances in which the original sentences are of different type. Consider the following sequence: 'Jimmy Carter once grew peanuts (declarative). Does Jimmy Carter like peanuts? (interrogative)'. In the embedded case this becomes 'Does Jimmy Carter who once grew peanuts like them?', with the force of a question, and this accords with our suggestion. But the rule suggested for embedding would, in the case of conjoining, lead to conflict when the original sentences are of different type. Consequently, the conjoined construction 'Jimmy Carter once grew peanuts and does he like them' is unacceptable. We should not, however, draw the general conclusion that sentences of different type may not be conjoined. For, 'Come closer!' (jussive) and 'I'll tell you a story' (declarative) may be conjoined to give 'Come closer and I'll tell you a story', a sentence that may be used to realise an illocutionary act, the force of which would be that of a mand. But what rule determines that the illocutionary force *will* be that of a mand? Does the force associated with the use of such a construction take the value associated with its first conjunct, for example?

A difficulty with this simple solution emerges when we consider another similar construction, which is also used to realise a mand, 'Come closer and I'll shoot!' where the first conjunct would not seem to have derived from the jussive sentence 'Come closer!' except possibly in the case of a

deliberate attempt at irony on the part of the addressor. It
seems rather to be an example of a class of 'pseudo-imperatives'
(cf. Jespersen 1946),[9] being equivalent to the conditional
'If you come closer, I'll shoot'.[10] The verb 'come', in other
words, is in the indicative mood, not the imperative, choice
of mood being determined in accordance with the meaning
of 'shoot' in the second conjunct. In the light of this observation we see now that the mood of the verb 'come' in our
earlier example 'Come closer and I'll tell you a story', was
ambiguous, since both the indicative and the imperative were
compatible with the meaning of the second conjunct in that
case. The force of such a construction would not seem then
to be determined by a rule that simply associates it with the
first conjunct, which in the given example is ambiguous in
that respect. Does it take the value associated with the second
conjunct? During our consideration of this question we will
return to the discussion of the co-ordination of verbal and iso-
verbal acts in conversation.

Continuing with the 'come closer' examples, we find that
the ambiguity regarding the mood of the verb 'come' may be
resolved by choice of intonation contour. Thus our first
example may be rendered as 'Come clòser and I'll tell you
a stòry' where intonation seems to select the imperative
mood, or as 'Come clóser and I'll tell you a stòry' where it
seems to select the indicative.[11] Now it is unlikely that in
selecting the mood of the verb intonation operates at a lexical
level. For one thing the stress falls on the adverb 'closer'.
A clue to how the selection mechanism may work is to be
found from a consideration of the tone sequences that could
be employed for the second rendering of this example. Tone
3 followed by tone 1 would certainly be appropriate for a
co-ordinate construction. On the other hand the sequence
might well be 4,1. Such a rendering would suggest the close
affinity of this construction with the conditional 'If you
come clóser, I'll tell you a stòry', which consists of a dependent
clause followed by its main clause (cf. Halliday 1970b:30).
By the choice of sequence 4,1 then the first conjunct would
be treated 'as if' it were a dependent 'if' clause, one whose
verb would be in the indicative mood. The second conjunct
by this account would act as the main clause. The outcome

would be a construction that, as signalled by tone 1 on the 'main' clause, is of the declarative type. But it may nonetheless be used to realise an illocutionary act whose *indirect* force would be that of a mand. The sequence 3,1 seems the appropriate one to choose for the other example 'Come closer and I'll shoot', despite the conditional (cf. Halliday, op. cit.). But the choice of tone 1 for the first conjunct would in this case sound ironic.The difference across these examples in the appropriate choice of tone for the first conjunct agrees with the interpretation of the first example as an 'invitation' and the second as a 'threat'.

Pending further data of the type presented by Sag and Liberman (op. cit.) we conclude for the moment that the literal force associated with the use of a compound sentence is expounded by the type III iso-verbal act that accompanies its main clause. But to the extent that the literal force may be required as input to a rule for the computation of the indirect force in some given context of use, they are reliable indicators of the addressor's communicative intention. Their function is clearly interaction-regulating. Iso-verbal acts, type III, are functionally equivalent to syntactic indicators of illocutionary force and may therefore replace them in conversational discourse.[12] Being a phenomenon of the audio-vocal medium of expression they are an integral part of the performance of spoken verbal acts, although they do not combine with them in a structural sense. Moreover, a number of variations may be superimposed on the 'basic' contour associated with a given verbal act. One set of variations alters the relevance of the act to its context (cf. Gunter, op. cit.), whilst variations of another type (vocal gestures) provide part of the vocal means for performing indexical acts, and these we will comment upon shortly.

We have seen that when two sentences combine a single illocutionary act results, the propositional components becoming embedded or conjoined. Now, iso-verbal acts are non-verbal realisations of illocutions: they convey a propositional meaning and/or a communicative intention. But the combination of propositions from a verbal and an iso-verbal act, type I or II, would be ruled out on structural grounds, and the two acts would consequently remain separate even if performed simultaneously. There would not appear therefore to be any structural constraints on the co-occurrence of verbal and iso-verbal acts. Are there any other constraints? A number of possibilities spring to mind, which group under the following headings: i) functional equivalence; ii) competition for the behavioural media of expression; iii) processing capacity, and iv) thematic continuity. A full examination of these would make for a very long discussion. In the context of this introduction, however, it will be appropriate to keep our comments brief and illustrative only.

The concept of 'functional equivalence' provides a principled basis for examining the co-occurrence of verbal and iso-verbal acts. For the present, given the uncharted nature of this area, we will simply formulate a working hypothesis, one that might provide a base from which to project experiments. Such a hypothesis is that a verbal act and an iso-verbal act, type I or II, may be performed simultaneously in co-operative conversation only if they are being used to realise or indicate the same illocutionary act, only if they are functionally equivalent, in other words. Examples are: beckoning (type I) whilst saying 'Come here!' and a type II manual gesture together with 'After you!'. Co-occurrence of a verbal act with a type II iso-verbal act would, accordingly, provide a means for assigning an interpretation to the latter. An undesirable feature of the hypothesis, however, is that co-occurrence of this type would appear simply to make iso-verbal acts redundant on such occasions of use, and redundancy is not an acceptable property of co-operative conversation (cf. Grice 1975). Resolution of this difficulty concerning the hypothesis must await the outcome of experiments designed to test it against the alternative hypothesis, namely, that functionally *in*equivalent pairs of verbal and iso-verbal acts may co-occur. But there are 'a priori' grounds for disfavouring the alternative hypothesis, as we will find from even a cursory look at the other types of constraint.

An obvious constraint on co-occurrence is set by competition for the behavioural media of expression. For example, use of the supra-laryngeal mechanism of articulation in the performance of verbal acts rules out its simultaneous use for the performance of iso-verbal acts, types I and II. It is not possible to perform the type I act 'Shh!' for example, whilst uttering 'Be quiet!' or, indeed, whilst vocally performing any other verbal act: this constraint operates equally with regard to both hypotheses. Another type of constraint, 'processing capacity', is evocative of the 'channel capacity hypothesis' of cognitive theory, except that 'limited capacity' in this case would be defined semiotically. We might hypothesise that two functionally *in*equivalent acts impose a greater processing load than two functionally equivalent acts. Such a hypothesis is readily testable. Related to the processing capacity constraint is what we may refer to as the 'thematic continuity rule' whereby both addressor and addressee must keep track of the same 'point-of-reference' (cf. Isard 1975a). The co-occurrence of two different illocutionary acts would result in two different up-datings of the point-of-reference, thereby creating the risk of thematic non-continuity. We conclude that an addressor may perform only one illocutionary act at a time in conversational discourse, but that it may be realised simultaneously by both verbal and iso-verbal means, provided this does not result in competition for the same behavioural medium of expression.[13]

Verbal and Indexical Acts

Let us turn now to the co-ordination of verbal and indexical acts, acts that we have so far characterised simply in terms of the addressor's internal state. The distinction between information about internal states and information about the environment has often been invoked in discussions of infant communication and in comparisons of communication in animals and man. Although this distinction may not always be readily drawn when considering verbal acts (cf. a comment of Hinde 1974: 142, and his example: 'I am afraid - - - (of) - - - a predator behind that tree'), we have supposed that indexical acts, on the other hand, only give expression to the addressor's internal state. But on further reflection, certain problems arise, which force us to revise our characterisation of indexical acts. We will examine these problems before moving on to consider the co-ordination of indexical acts with verbal acts during conversation.

One problem, which we have already touched upon, concerns the distinction between 'affective indices' (Abercrombie 1967) and what MacKay (1972) and Lyons (1972) refer to as 'symptoms'. Symptoms are exemplified by what Abercrombie (1967) described as 'indices which accompany conditions such as fatigue, excitement, catarrh, grief, over-consumption of alcohol, nervousness'. He writes that indices of this type have a 'direct physical cause', in contrast to *affective* indices, which do not. According to Abercrombie it is from affective indices rather than symptoms that we infer such feelings as amusement, anger, contempt, sympathy, and suspicion. Affective indices may be carried by both the audible medium of expression, when they constitute 'tone of voice', and the visible, when the affect is manifested as an 'affect display' (Ekman and Friesen 1969). Affect displays are those expressions (primarily facial) of internal states that Ekman and Friesen associate with the 'primary affects' of happiness, surprise, fear, sadness, anger, disgust and interest. Whilst each of the primary affects may be associated with an underlying display which is 'universal to mankind', the surface display is determined according to culture-specific 'display rule norms' and is not therefore related to the affect causally, at least in the sense of 'causal' implied in Abercrombie's usage. We will not concern ourselves further with the difficult issue of causality, however, but turn now to two related questions concerning our characterisation of indexical acts: i) does an act which conveys affective indices necessarily count in our terms as an indexical act, and ii) need the affective indices conveyed by an interactive act be accompanied by corresponding inner states for it to count as an indexical act?

Some examples may help to illuminate these questions. Consider the following instances of a *smile*, this being a common affect display:

i)   *A* is walking towards someone whom he thinks might be an acquaintance he has not seen for years. She suddenly recognises him and *smiles* (Hello! What a lovely surprise!). He *smiles* back and continues walking towards her.

ii) *A* is at an airport, queuing at the information desk. When his turn comes the information officer faces him and *smiles* (May I help you?). *A* puts his question.

iii)   *A* and *B* are talking about a problem that has arisen in *B*'s research, when a solution suddenly occurs to *A*, and he says 'I've got it!' and looks at *B*. *B smiles* (Good! What is it?). *A* explains his solution.

iv)   *A* is chatting with his wife and comments that he feels like some coffee, hoping that she will go and make it. She *smiles* (That would be nice, provided you make it.) *A* says 'Alright, *I'll* go and make it', and goes to the kitchen.

Now, our first question concerns the criteria whereby a smile, for example, may count as an *interactive* act? (The verbal glosses in parentheses are of course, illustrative only, being intended to capture the 'meaning' of the smile in each case). But first, what do we mean by 'interactive'? Since the concept deserves a chapter to itself, we will not attempt a summary review here. We will simply take the definitions offered by Ekman and Friesen (1969), MacKay (1972) and Scheflen (1975), and adjust them to suit our own purposes.

According to Ekman and Friesen, interactive acts 'clearly modify or influence the interactive behaviour' of a recipient. The recursive use of the term 'interactive' in their definition is implicit also in Scheflen's: 'In the interactional event the behaviour of one participant influences the next behaviour of at least one other participant, and this influence in turn is discernible in whatever comes next'. In order to avoid an infinite regress, however, we will rather try to define the interactive act in terms that are of lower logical type than the term 'interactive' itself, whilst at the same time retaining the underlying principles of interdependency and reciprocity captured in these authors' definitions. To this end we will invoke MacKay's analysis of the related concepts: 'informative act' and 'communicative act'.[14] Taking his concepts in their re-packed form we will describe an act by person *A* as 'informative' if it produces an effect on *B*, and 'communicative' if *A* intends[15] in performing it to produce a given effect on *B and B* recognises that intention. The second part of our definition of 'communicative act' is not included in that of Ekman and Friesen, the major difference between their definition and ours being therefore that according to theirs a communicative act, in order to count as such, need not be 'consummated' (cf. Searle 1969), and this may indeed be the case with infant intentional acts. By our definition, the illocutionary act may be treated as a special kind of communicative act, one in which it is also A's 'reflexive intention' (cf. Grice 1957) that B should recognise his intention to produce the given effect. A may secure that recognition by his use of a 'conventional expression' (verbal or non-verbal). We will extend our use of the term 'communicative intention' so that it is applicable within the broader context of our definition of the communicative act, whereby it is A's communicative intention to have the effect on B that he recognise what illocutionary act was performed and what it is A wants him to do or believe. Earlier we used the term in a more restrictive sense,[16] in order to keep the discussion manageable at that point. A and B in our definitions correspond to 'addressor' and 'addressee' respectively (see Halliday's comment, this Symposium, concerning the phenomenon of 'address'). We have been using these terms rather than 'sender' and 'recipient' in order i) to restrict our discussion to that kind of reciprocal behaviour between A and B in which each is the 'target' of the other's communicative act (see MacKay 1972: 20) and ii) to exclude from discussion here the phenomenon called 'idle listening' by Miller and Johnson-Laird (1976: 202ff). We will now define the 'interactive act' as a communicative act that is i) contingent upon the recognition by the addressor of the communicative intention conveyed to him by the addressee during the preceding turn and/or ii) is reciprocated with a similarly interdependent act by the addressee during the following turn. An interactive act then is one that is influenced by a preceding communicative act if there is one, and in turn, influences the next in the way broadly described by Scheflen. In our definition we have tried to capture what may be the mechanism whereby such a sequence is generated.

Can we now, in the light of the distinctions we have drawn, decide which of our four instances of a smile may be counted as interactive acts? In his discussion of an example similar to our first, Hinde (1974) described it as 'spontaneous' and 'non-directed' (i.e., unintentional). Is our first example then

to be taken as a non-interactive act? To examine this question
we might begin by considering whether the acquaintance
would have smiled in the same way had she known that *A*
had not yet noticed her. It seems unlikely that she would
have done, any affect displayed in that event being derived
perhaps from the 'basic affect programs' (Ekman and Friesen)
associated with her inner states of happiness and surprise.
The resulting display might *inform* an un-addressed observer
of her feelings, but it could not have been intended to produce
an effect on *A*. On the other hand, in the case instanced,
where the acquaintance would have known that *A* had seen,
if not recognised her, her smile is, we suggest, one which
results primarily from the operation of those 'display rules'
(Ekman and Friesen) that in her culture are appropriate for
the performance of the communicative act of greeting an
acquaintance. This is not to deny that there will be a component of the total display corresponding to her felt happiness
and surprise, one which adds 'spontaneity' to her smile. We
would simply propose that this component is 'blended' with
the greeting component, and that it is the latter which gives
to the smile its interactive potential. If we now take *A*'s
smile to be contingent upon his recognition of the acquaintance's
intention to greet him, rather than treat it as a symptom of
his own inner states of happiness and surprise on seeing her,
then both the initiating smile and the responding smile will
count in our terms as interactive acts. Such a greeting sequence
provides a familiar example of the 'adjacency pair' (Schegloff
and Sacks 1973).

Our first example of the smile seemed *a priori* the one least
likely to qualify as an interactive act. Having concluded that
it *is*, we will assume that the other three would also emerge from
such scrutiny as interactive acts. But now, do our examples
of the smile count as instances of *indexical* acts? This brings
us to the second of the two questions we put earlier. We can
illustrate our answer with the airport example. The smile of the
information officer may be regarded as a means for effecting
a smooth transition to *A* from the previous consultant. We
need not assume any accompanying affect, however, unless
A unexpectedly turned out to be an acquaintance, in which
case the smile may have the 'spontaneity' of our first example,

and be accompanied perhaps, by an 'eye-brow flash' of recognition and surprise (cf. Eibl-Eibesfeldt 1972). The smile in this example conveys something like: 'Now, I shall be pleased to help you' or 'May I (have the pleasure of) help(ing) you?', whether or not the information officer expects to feel pleased. Either way, according to our revised definition (below) the smile in this case will count as an indexical act. In other words, the affective indices carried by an indexical act in adult social behaviour are separable from those internal states to which they may originally (in the ontogenetic sense) have pointed. The affect may be 'simulated', as in those instances where a correlated internal state is absent, or 'dissimulated', as in those instances where, whilst an *un*-correlated internal state is present, the addressor intends to keep it hidden. Onset of the ability to perform indexical acts independently of underlying affect must surely be an important milestone in the development of the child's capacity for social interaction.

We are now in a position to formulate a simple, working definition of the indexical act: it is a non-verbal interactive act bearing affective indices, which do not necessarily correlate with internal (affective) states. The revised definition extends the use of the term to include instances in which, though the affective indices are not correlated with the addressor's feelings they constitute a conventional signal, which may be used to serve a social-emotional function. Our four examples of the smile come into the class so defined. In the first the smile serves as a greeting. In the second it plays perhaps a mildly propitiatory role, in that failure to smile in this context might be seen to be abrupt and unfriendly. In the third the smile indicates *B*'s approval, and this is taken by *A* as an *implicit* invitation to explain his solution. The fourth example illustrates a more subtle use of the smile. *A*'s comment is both intended and recognised by his wife as an indirect request for her to make some coffee. She also would like some coffee, but wants him to make it. She therefore countermands his indirect request by responding with an implicit request of her own. Her smile conveys something like 'That would be nice, provided you make it'. *A* correctly interprets her manoeuvre and complies, albeit ungraciously.

Given our revised definition, can we take the indexical act to be a non-verbal realisation of an illocutionary act? That is, does it have a propositional content and/or an illocutionary force? We will illustrate our approach to this question by continuing to examine our examples of the smile. Now clearly the smile in each case does not express the meaning of the corresponding gloss. We inferred that meaning largely from the verbal context. Nevertheless, some interpretation of the smile must have been a part of the procedure whereby the inference was made. For, if the smile were replaced with a frown, for example, the gloss would then be inappropriate. So what meaning, if any, does the smile express? A hypothesis we will now examine is that the smile in each of our examples is a non-verbal expression of that 'propositional function' that could be expressed verbally as '(be) pleased/happy', a function that, when expressed by a smile, is predicated of the addressor. Thus, when asked 'Are you happy today?', *A* might respond by both nodding his head and smiling to convey 'Yes, I am happy'. Given the context provided by the question, this meaning could, of course, be inferred from the head-nod alone, and the smile may be treated as a gratuitous act. But he could also give this response to the question 'Is your wife happy today?', when it would seem to convey the meaning of 'Yes, I am happy *to say*'. In this case a head-nod on its own could only convey the meaning of 'Yes, *my wife is happy*'. Therefore, the part of the meaning corresponding to '*I* am happy' could only have been conveyed, if at all, by smiling. However, merely to say 'Yes, I am happy' in response to the question would be inappropriate. And so smiling appears to convey more in this context than does the saying of 'I am happy/pleased'. Indeed, in our earlier examples the proposition 'I (be) happy/pleased' was not even a part of the meaning for any of the accompanying glosses. Our choice of a verbal gloss in each of those examples was of course to some extent arbitrary. Nevertheless, our choices did seem at least more appropriate than the gloss: 'I am happy/pleased'. But now, we could replace the glosses accompanying those examples with the following, which do appear to be appropriate: 'I am pleased *to see you*'; 'I shall be pleased *to help you*'; 'I would be pleased *to hear your solution*',

and 'I would be pleased *if you made the coffee*'. The exact
wording of the glosses is not important. What we are doing
here is simply making explicit a distinction between that
part of the total meaning conveyed, which we hypothesise
to be expressed by smiling, 'I (be) pleased',[17] and that part,
corresponding to the portions in italics, which may be inferred
from the context. Of course we cannot express the meanings
of these glosses by simply smiling and saying only the parts
in italics. But this could be largely a matter of structural
constraints operating against the combination of verbal and
non-verbal elements in the performance of an interactive
act. It has no direct bearing on the hypothesis that the smile
predicates '(be) pleased/happy' of the addressor. We begin to
get a lever on the hypothesis when we compare the new
glosses with the ones we gave earlier.

Consider our third example of the smile. The glosses, 'I
would be pleased to hear it' and 'Good! What is it?' are associated with different illocutionary acts, different in terms of
their propositional content at least. What then is the basis
of our judgement that they are both appropriate, given the
context? To answer this question we must look below the
surface of the acts performed by *A* and *B*. Having announced
that he has a solution, *A* looks at *B* for encouragement to go
on and explain it. *B* smiles at *A*, and in doing so in the given
context, indicates (whether or not he feels it) that he is pleased
A has found a solution. He intends that *A* will recognise this
indication of approval as an implicit invitation to explain
his solution. *A* does recognise *B*'s intention and proceeds with
his explanation. Now, this description of what is going on
below the surface results from using only the first setting
of our analytical microscope. We would need to increase the
power considerably if we wanted to unpack such descriptive
place-holders as 'encouragement', 'approval' and 'implicit'
invitation'. But this level of description will suffice to give
an indication at least, of the non-linguistic procedures underlying the 'felicitous' performance of an indexical act, such as
the smile in our example. If the analysis is correct, it provides
a rational basis for determing the appropriateness of our two
glosses: they both convey *B*'s *underlying intention*. In other
words, saying either 'I would be pleased to hear it' or 'Good!

what is it?' would perform the same communicative act as the one performed in this context by smiling. Like the smile, they each convey approval. But, unlike the smile, they make *ex*plicit the invitation that is only *im*plicit in the conveyance of approval.

Let us try now to evaluate the hypothesis that the smile in those instances we have discussed expresses the proposition corresponding to 'I (be) pleased', call it *P*. But first, let us be clear about the possible outcomes of the attempt to do so. Confirmation would have a direct bearing on the question with which we began this section, namely, whether indexical acts may be functionally equivalent to the verbal realisation of an illocutionary act. For, as we noted earlier, a proposition may not be expressed except in the performance of an illocutionary act (Searle 1969: 29). Disconfirmation, on the other hand, would be an ambiguous outcome in that smiling either realises an illocutionary act that does not have *P* as its propositional content, or that does not have *any* propositional content, or it does not realise an illocutionary act. The possibilities associated with this outcome comprise the set of 'null' hypotheses.

To facilitate the evaluation, let us summarise our observations concerning the smile as follows: i) simply to say 'I (be) pleased' does not convey the same underlying intention as that conveyed by the smile; ii) that intention could however be conveyed in each instance by means of a verbal act that includes an expression of *P*, but iii) that same intention could also be conveyed by a verbal act that does *not* include an expression of *P*. What conclusions may we draw from these observations concerning the hypothesis? At first glance, observation (i) on its own provides sufficient grounds for rejecting the hypothesis. For if smiling and saying 'I (be) pleased' were expressions of the same proposition, would they not convey the same underlying intention when performed in the same context? We may parry this thrust at the hypothesis by pointing out that the same proposition may be expressed in the performance of different illocutionary acts, and that it could be the latter difference that accounts for observation (i). From observations (ii) and (iii) however, comes the riposte that different illocutionary acts may nevertheless convey the *same* underlying intention. Consequently, even if the underlying intentions conveyed by smiling and saying 'I (be) pleased' *were* the same, we still could not conclude that they realise the same illocutionary act and that they incorporate therefore an expression of the same proposition.

And so our observations do not lead to an unambiguous confirmation of the hypothesis that the smile in our examples expresses *P*, and we must reject it in favour of one of the null hypotheses. We will defer choosing among these until after we have looked more closely at our use of the terms 'express' and 'underlying intention'.

During our evaluation of the hypothesis we ran into the problem that the chain of inference from the underlying intention conveyed in the performance of an indexical act to the proposition it might be said to express is broken, because more than one illocutionary act may be used to convey that intention (sic: observations (ii) and (iii)). But it is not clear in what sense the term 'express' is being used here. A major problem when discussing the non-verbal expression of a proposition is that propositions are closely related to the *sentences* used to express them (cf. Lyons, this Symposium). In order to talk about the proposition associated with the performance of a non-verbal act we have to 'translate' the non-verbal expression of it into a verbal one. In the case of an iso-verbal act, type I, this presents little difficulty. In the case of the smile however, we were not able to make a direct translation and had to resort, unsuccessfully, to a process of inference. That being the case, we are nudged towards the conclusion that the smile does not express a proposition. Let us, in fact, propose that in performing a communicative act, an addressor may be said to express a proposition only if the pairing of the act and the proposition is determined according to 'convention'.[18] Then if an act expressed a proposition we would be able to translate it. Since we cannot do so in the case of the smile, it may not be said to express a proposition. That is, whereas an utterance of the sentence 'I am pleased' is a conventional means for expressing *P*, smiling is not. And so, we arrive at a point where the question whether it is a general feature of indexical acts that they express propositions is an empirical one. We must find out if there is *agreement* regarding the translation. Should it prove to be the case that indexical acts do not express propositions, however, which in further discussion we will now take to be the case, we still would not have ruled out the possibility that they may realise illocutionary acts. We will pursue this point, together with an examination of our use of the term 'underlying intention'.

In our discussion of the third example of the smile we stated that B intended that A would recognise his indication of approval as an implicit invitation to explain his solution. This was an instance of what we have been calling an 'underlying intention'. A recognised B's intention, and the smile, therefore, counted as a communicative act. It conveyed the underlying intention. Now, A's recognition of the underlying intention was contingent upon his recognition of B's approval. B could have made his approval explicit by employing a conventional expression of approval, such as 'Good!', in which case we could have said that B had performed an illocutionary act. A would have recognised B's approval, that is, in virtue of his knowledge of the convention. But how *was* that recognition achieved?[19] Observation (ii) provides something of a clue. Although the act of smiling in our examples did not express P, there appeared to be something in common to them all, which is reflected in the fact that we could incorporate P into an appropriate gloss in each case. But the 'something in common' is not analysable in propositional terms. We cannot reduce the meaning of an indexical act to the psychological correlates of a world comprised of first and second-order entities. An analysis in terms of a 'representational model' of meaning (cf. Halliday 1973:16), which is appropriate in the case of verbal and iso-verbal acts, does not seem to work for indexical acts. The model is inapplicable even in the case of some verbal acts. Thus, in saying 'Ouch!' I do not express the proposition corresponding to 'That hurt!', though my utterance may constitute a complaint to the effect that something hurts. Similarly, though smiling does not express the proposition 'I (be) pleased', it may nevertheless constitute a conventional means for performing an *act of approval* (like clapping or cheering). If, with Searle, we accept the saying of 'Ouch!' and 'Hurrah!' as illocutionary acts, it would seem but a small step to accept that the smile might also be used to perform an illocutionary act. We suggest that it may function as a *literal* illocutionary act of approval, and as such may be used to perform a number of *indirect* illocutionary acts, such as a greeting (first example); a propitiation (second example); an invitation (third example) and, by its ironic use, a request (fourth example). The intention associated with the indirect illocutionary act is what we have been calling the 'underlying intention'.

Our discussion has led us to select from the set of 'null' hypotheses the one according to which the smile, when performed in a context of the type we have illustrated, may realise an illocutionary act that has no propositional content. This hypothesis may now be raised to the status of an 'experimental hypothesis' for the purpose of empirical evaluation. A possibly fruitful line of investigation would begin by examining the co-occurrence of indexical and verbal interactive acts. In this respect, indexical acts may be quite different from iso-verbal acts. As we have seen, they are not readily translatable into verbal acts with which they could be said to stand in a relation of 'functional equivalence'. Consequently, the 'processing capacity' constraint that we mooted at a corresponding point in our discussion of iso-verbal acts, may not apply, or, at least, may operate quite differently in the case of indexical acts. Moreover, given they have no propositional content, their simultaneous performance with verbal acts should not create problems of 'thematic non-continuity' for the addressee. Further, unlike iso-verbal acts, types I and II, the indexical act is not subject to a constraint on medium-sharing with the verbal act it accompanies. In fact, medium-sharing in the case of 'tone of voice', provides for the precise co-ordination of an indexical act with a selected component of the verbal act it accompanies. Consider an utterance of the sentence 'She walked across the Meadows' in answer to the question 'Which way did she go home from the party?'. By accompanying the first syllable of 'Meadows' with a certain 'vocal gesture' or shift of 'register', or both, the addressor is able to indicate his surprise that the woman in question did not avoid, at night, at area of Edinburgh in which muggings have been known to occur. In this example, where the indexical act coincides with the 'tonic syllable' (Halliday 1970b) of the associated verbal act, its effect on the underlying intention conveyed may be analysed in terms of an elaboration of the semantic interpretation corresponding to the 'focus' (Chomsky 1969). But indexical acts may elaborate the meanings of the verbal acts they accompany in a variety of ways that provide a rich potential for altering the under-lying intentions conveyed. However, even a cursory look at some of these ways would be beyond our present scope.

The difference between indexical and iso-verbal acts, with respect to the constraints on their co-occurrence with verbal acts is, as we have just seen, quite sharp. The difference in functional terms is correspondingly clean-cut. Whilst iso-verbal acts, types I and II, serve mainly an ideational-informative function, and type III an interaction-regulating function, indexical acts serve mainly a social-emotional function in conversation.

Summary and Conclusion

Our treatment of non-verbal behaviour has isolated for discussion only the part that may be described as the non-verbal com-ponent of conversational interactivity. We subdivided this component into three types of interactive acts: iso-verbal, indexical and meta-communicative, and argued that an act of either of the first two types may realise an illocution. But whereas we may ascribe propositional content to an iso-verbal act, we are unable to do so in the case of an indexical act. Moreover, whilst iso-verbal acts are functionally equivalent to verbal acts, into which they may readily be translated, indexical acts are not. Correspondingly, we find differences with respect to four constraints on their co-occurrence with verbal acts: i) functional equivalence; ii) thematic continuity; iii) processing capacity, and iv) competition for the media of expression. Accordingly, they are different in terms of their meaning-relationships with the verbal acts they accompany. Whereas the meaning of the iso-verbal act is correlated with the meaning of the co-occurring verbal act, that of the indexical act may supplement or even contradict it. Consequently, although in the case of co-occurrence with an iso-verbal act the communicative intention conveyed is the same as it would be if the verbal act were performed on its own, in the case of the indexical act it may be quite different. Indexical acts may, indeed, provide a subtle means for modifying or elaborating upon the underlying intention conveyed in the performance of the same verbal act in different contexts. Occasionally iso-verbal acts (types I and II) and indexical acts occur in sequence with verbal acts, in which instances the intention conveyed is determined according to convention in the case of iso-verbal acts (type I) and, in the case of indexical acts (and iso-verbal acts, type II), in part by convention and in part pragmatically according to context. Indexical and iso-verbal acts differ also in gross functional terms. Indexical acts provide a rich source of control over the social-emotional relationship between addressor and addressee. Iso-verbal acts (types I and II) on the other hand, accompany in a 'non-obligato' role, the verbal exchange of ideas, whilst type III has an important interaction-regulating function. Meta-communicative acts, which comprise our third type of non-verbal acts, have received extensive treatment in the literature, albeit under various descriptive labels, and have not therefore been pursued further here. But they provide an important supplement to the linguistic devices for text-construction described by some of the contributors to the Symposium (cf. Halliday, Lyons and Widdowson). These three types of interactive acts comprise the non-verbal component of the reciprocal behaviour that generates conversation. Having looked at the question concerning their co-ordination with the verbal acts of conversation, we will now, by way of a conclusion, take a brief look at the part that two of them, the iso-verbal and the indexical, may play in the developmental shift to verbal interactivity.

An approach to the question concerning this developmental shift, within the descriptive framework of 'speech-act theory' has been outlined recently by Bates (1976); Bruner (1975, 1976) and Dore (1974, 1975).[20] According to Bates, statements and mands are pre-figured non-verbally during the later part of the sensorimotor period (Stage 5) of cognitive development. Such *proto-statements* and *proto-mands*[21] are not, however, functionally equivalent to verbal interactive acts. They are 'pure performatives',[22] lacking in propositional content. According to Bates, the insertion of propositions into these 'performative frames' must await development of the capacity for 'internal representation', at sensorimotor Stage 6. Prior to this development therefore, the pointing gesture, for example, resembles the corresponding type I iso-verbal act in form only. It does not function yet as an act of *proto-reference*. Once this function has been established, however, the act may be realised by means of new forms, for example, the verbal expressions 'that' and 'there'. We are suggesting then, that an iso-verbal act may provide a 'bridge' for the developmental shift from the pointing gesture to verbal acts of reference ('that' or 'there'). The subsequent role of *deixis* in the development of conversation and discourse provided a main theme of the Symposium. Other type I acts, for example, the non-verbal equivalents of saying 'yes' and 'no', may follow a similar devopmental course. In the case of type II acts, the context-sensitive relation that obtains, by definition, between the illocutionary act and the signal realising it, marks this hypothetical type as a candidate for the characterization of an intermediate stage in the development of type I, but we will avoid any further speculation on this possibility and turn now to a brief consideration of type III and indexical acts.

Directing our attention first to the part that indexical acts may play in the development of conversation, we will look at some implications of the findings of individual differences in interactional style among children at the earlier stages of language use. For example, Nelson (1973) identified two groups of children, a 'referential' group who were object-oriented, and an 'expressive' group who were self-oriented. The distinction corresponds broadly to that between our F1 (ideational-informative) and F2 (social-emotional) functions. And these are associated in turn, with our iso-verbal acts (type I/II) and indexical acts. But what was the developmental history of the observed differences in interactional style? Can it be traced back to the earliest phases of mother-infant interaction? The result of a simple 'gedanken' experiment would seem to rule out that possibility. For, supposing we were to trace the development of Nelson's two groups backward, in the way described by Bullowa (this Symposium), to a stage where interactive acts are performed non-verbally. To the extent that non-verbal interactivity is to be characterised in terms of iso-verbal and indexical acts, the referential-expressive distinction would vanish at sensorimotor Stage 5, the capacity to perform iso-verbal acts (types I and II, at least) being contingent on the capacity for performing pro-positional acts at the later, representational Stage 6. That is, differences in interactional *style* in the pre-verbal stage are, by this account, contingent on a certain level of *cognitive* development.

According to the way we have characterised the differences between iso-verbal acts (type I/II) and indexical acts then, and assuming the validity of the cited distinction between sensori-motor Stages 5 and 6, indexical acts would have the longer developmental history. In fact, as a purely conceptual vehicle, the indexical act may enable us to travel, in theory at least, as far as the ontogenetic source of conversation, when com-munication is dedicated to the I-thou relationship described by Bullowa. Of course, the theory needs putting to the test. But let us postpone for just a little longer our giddy return to the laboratory (or the home) in order to look at the role of iso-verbal acts, type III, in the early development of con-versation.

In a related study to that of Nelson, Dore (1974) observed a difference in interactional style between a 'word baby' who was object-oriented, and an 'intonation baby' who was 'person-oriented'. The difference corresponds again to our F1-F2 distinction, except that F2 would seem to require sub-dividing in order to capture the distinction between self-oriented and (other) person-oriented acts of communication. Person-oriented acts included 'request (action)' 'request (answer)', and 'call', which were conveyed by a 'constant' contour, a rising contour, and a rising-falling contour respec-tively. Such contours are of the type that we associate with the performance of iso-verbal acts, type III.

But now, two important questions arise concerning the use of intonation contour at this stage of development: i) Is there a within-child consistency in the relationship between contour and illocutionary force? and ii) Is there a corresponding between-child consistency? One small comparison suggests

that the answer to the second of these questions may be
'No'. For, whereas Dore's subject 'M'[23] is said to have indicated
the force of a 'request (answer)' by means of a rising contour,
[buk], Nigel at about the same age (15 months), employed
a falling contour: [aːːdà] (Halliday 1975, and this Symposium).
However, this example does not provide unambiguous evidence
that children differ in the way they use intonation contour
for indicating illocutionary force. We could argue alternatively,
that the difference in contour marks a difference in 'rank'[24]
between the two acts; that Nigel, who knew the answer, may
simply have been performing the *initiating move* of a ritual
exchange in the 'naming game', whilst 'M' on the other hand,
may have been performing one of the 'conversational'
acts' (see p.17) that may be used to realise the initiating
move of a conversational exchange, namely, an *elicitation*.[25]
But she could not have been realising the elicitation itself by
means of a yes/no question since this would call for further
linguistic development. Or would it? This brings us to question
(iii) below.

Before pursuing questions (i) and (ii) any further, there is
a third to consider, which is logically prior to both of them.
That is: iii) Do the major categories of illocutionary force
have their counterparts in pre-linguistic communication?
Our reason for raising this question concerns an important
property of iso-verbal acts, type III, not shared with the
other non-verbal acts we have discussed,[26] that they are
linguistically organized. As we pointed out earlier, they have
the linguistic function of expounding those categories of
illocutionary force that correspond to the major sentence
types. At this point therefore, we are led to ask whether
these categories are 'intrinsic to language' (cf. Halliday 1975)
and, if so, whether the corresponding 'communication roles'
of *telling, asking, requesting* and *ordering*, and the like, may
only be played linguistically. For, if that were the case, would
we not conclude straightaway that the answer to question
(iii) is 'no'? We are not, in fact, driven to that conclusion by
logical necessity. Indeed, cogent and empirically-based argu-
ments have been presented on both sides (cf. Bloom 1973
and Dore 1975). And additional evidence unfortunately, has
not enabled us to resolve the issue, as we shall now see.

In his study, Halliday (op. cit.) did not find a direct relationship between Nigel's 'phase I' (9-15 months) functions and
the communication roles of adult conversation. Moreover,
when Nigel began, in his twentieth month, systematically
to use the contrast between rising and falling tones, it served
to distinguish acts 'demanding a response' ('pragmatic')
from ones that did not ('mathetic'). And this use does not
correspond in any simple way to the one operating in the
adult system. Halliday's findings appear then, to favour the
negative answer to question (iii)[27]. On the other hand, an
affirmative answer finds support from the data of Bates and
her colleagues, who argued from their observations of two
children, Marta and Carlotta, that they both began to perform
proto-mands and proto-statements during the age range from
12-17 months, which corresponded for them to sensorimotor
Stage 5. But there was no evidence from this study bearing
on questions (i) or (ii). Moreover, in an investigation of question
(i), an affirmative answer to question (iii) being tacitly assumed,
Myers (1975) was unable to find a systematic relationship
between the tones used by one child, Christopher (9-22
months), and a classification of the corresponding vocalisations, by a panel of judges, into either the set of illocutionary acts listed by Searle (1969) or the phase I functions
of Halliday's system. But Christopher's learning of the mother
tongue was comparatively slow, so that even in the later
observation sessions, two-word utterances had hardly begun
to appear. There was no evidence, therefore, to suggest whether
major categories of illocutionary force are first marked syntactically, or by means of tone, or whether both types of
force-indicating devices appear simultaneously in development. And so, questions (i) - (iii) must all remain open for
the present.

Finally, and with respect to question (iii), we will continue
to maintain as a working hypothesis that children begin to perform proto-mands and proto-statements during the first half of
the second year (cf. Bates 1976; Dore 1974 and Myers 1975).
Although at that stage they may not have the means to adopt
and assign to others the communication roles that are associated
with verbal interactivity, they are able, we suggest, to express
precursors of those psychological states, namely 'belief' and

'desire (want)', that correspond to the sincerity condition for the performance of a statement and a mand, respectively (cf. Searle 1976). Accordingly, an adult addressee of such 'acts of meaning' (Halliday 1975 and this Symposium) may project onto them what Searle calls an 'illocutionary point', that the child is telling him how something is, or trying to get him to do something. A little earlier in development, when the child is unable to express these psychological states, in a way that is intelligible to others at least, his behaviour will not be seen to have either type of illocutionary point. But he may be able nonetheless to express feelings and attitudes (e.g. approval), which is the illocutionary point of the class of acts Searle calls 'expressives', and thereby to perform indexical acts.

Notes

1. Searle's steps for deriving the intended illocutionary force do not include his earlier 'essential condition' (Searle 1969), which is arguably semantic and not therefore allowable in a purely pragmatic solution. (cf. Katz 1972).
2. This term appears in my notes from the NATO Conference in Stirling on The Psychology of Language, against the name of Els Oksaar, though I have no recollection of how she may have used the term.
3. There are a number of differences between Key's classification and ours which should be noted. Our 'interactive acts' are described as 'behaviour events' in Key's System (K S); our iso-verbal acts are further differentiated into 'lexical' and 'descriptive' types of paralinguistic and kinesic acts in K S; we are not drawing a distinction between paralinguistic and kinesic acts, our classification being neutral with regard to behavioural media of expression (N.B. Key reserves the term 'paralinguistic' for vocalisations only); we are treating 'intonation' as an iso-verbal component rather than (as in K S), a 'verbal component' of the verbal act, and our classification into 'indexical' and 'meta-communicative' acts cuts across Key's 'reinforcing', 'embellishing' and 'incidental' types of non-verbal act. Some of the differences are simply a question of labelling, whilst others result from the different levels of description used in the two ystems. Our system differs also from that of Ekman and Friesen (1969) as we will point out in the body of the text (Section 3).
4. By 'context-of-interaction' we will, unless otherwise stated, be referring globally to the combined physical, social and linguistic factors that constrain the interpretation of interactive acts. We will not be drawing a distinction between 'context' and 'co-text'.
5. As an utterance it is of course ambiguous out of context, being transcribable as either 'no' or 'know'. Either way, however, it

would be recognised as a linguistic event. (See Austin 1962, for use of the term 'locutionary').

6. At this point we are using the term 'procedure' in the sense described by Widdowson (this Symposium), and 'pragmatic' in the sense employed by Bates (1976), who defines pragmatics as 'the study of linguistic indices, . . . (which) . . . can be interpreted only when they are used. One cannot describe the meanings of indices - one can only describe rules for relating them to contexts in which meanings can be found'.

7. The 'tonic' according to Halliday, marks the 'new' information. However the rules for the placement of the tonic are complex (see Schmerling 1976).

8. The three major types of discourse acts which realise an initiating move are *elicitation, informative* and *directive*, corresponding to question, statement and command respectively. The three corresponding types of act that occur in response are *reply, acknowledge* and *react* respectively. See Sinclair and Coulthard (1975).

9. My thanks here to Jim Miller for drawing my attention to the relevance of Jespersen's category of 'pseudo-imperatives' to this part of the discussion.

10. This example derives from Fillenbaum (1976), who contrasted the use of this sentence with that of another of similar type and construction: 'If you help me, I'll give you sixpence'. Whereas the first would be employed for issuing a 'threat', the second would convey an 'invitation'.

11. The notation we are using here merely draws the broad distinction between rising and falling tones. ⁄(rising) subsumes tones 2, 3 and 4, and ⟍ (falling) subsumes tones 1 and 5 in Halliday's system (see Halliday 1970b).

12. Moreover, where intonation signals a different force from that corresponding to the sentence type, as given syntactically, the 'functional classification' of the utterance will be determined by its intonation (Lyons 1972).

13. When as in the use of the American Sign Language, gestural signs are employed for constructing non-verbal equivalents of illocutionary acts, simultaneity, which is logically possible, does not usually occur in normal conversational use. 'The lexically specified subject or object of a predicate is not regularly expressed simultaneously with the sign for the predicate itself. We do find use of a deictic sign 'there' (index finger pointing to a locus in sign space) occurring simultaneously with a lexical sign (e.g., 'girl'), but two lexical signs do not ordinarily occur at the same time' (Klima and Bellugi 1975).

14. A 'communicative act' may be defined in terms of MacKay's (1972) analysis as: an act whose 'organizing function' in the 'recipient's meta-organizing system' is 'evaluated in the sender's meta-organizing system'.

15. MacKay translates 'intended' as: 'evaluated in the sender's meta-organizing system'.

16. Until now we have taken the addressor's 'communicative intention' to be recognition by the addressee of the illocutionary force with which the corresponding propositional act is per-

formed (see p.4). Dore (1977) takes it to be both recognition by the 'hearer' of the 'illocutionary status of the speaker's utterance' *and* his recognition of what it is the speaker expects him to do or believe as a consequence of recognising the illocutionary act.

17.   We will disregard the fact that the copula element 'be' is differently realised across our examples since it may be treated as a 'purely grammatical dummy' (Lyons 1968).

18.   The relationship between an expression and its literal meaning will be described as 'conventional' if it is *agreed* upon by the users of the expression.

19.   For ease of discussion we are arguing as if our examples derive from observation. But of course, they were constructed on the basis of intuition and therefore, require testing empirically.

20.   A comparison between this approach and that of Halliday (1973, 1975) was presented by Myers (1975).

21.   Bates (1976) refers to these as 'proto-declaratives' and 'proto-imperatives' respectively.

22.   Austin (1962) dropped the notion of 'the purity of performatives' himself, arguing that it derived from the unhappy distinction between constatives and performatives.

23.   'M' was, in fact, the 'word baby'.

24.   The term is being employed here in the manner of Sinclair and Coulthard (1975), who place in descending order of rank, 'exchange', 'move' and 'discourse act'.

25.   See note 8, where for 'discourse act' read 'conversational act'.

26.   In fact, tonic placement is also said to be linguistically organized (cf. Halliday 1970b and Crystal 1975), and this we have included within the category of meta-communicative acts (see p.12). But we have not discussed these here.

27.   However, as Halliday (1975) himself pointed out, the distinction between 'mathetic' and 'pragmatic' acts corresponds to Lewis's (1936) distinction between 'declarative' and 'manipulative' acts, which are usually taken to be of a 'response-expecting nature' (cf. Reeder, this Symposium p.116). Looked at from this perspective Nigel could be seen to have used tone at this stage to mark the distinction between proto-declaratives and proto-mands, and that interpretation would support an affirmative answer to both questions (i) and (iii). Accordingly, our argument would take a different tack.

INFANTS
AS CONVERSATIONAL PARTNERS

Introduction

It may seem quixotic to attribute conversation to infants since the concept of conversation seems to entail language and to presume that the conversationalists share social and linguistic skills. But the idea has some currency. Denzin, a sociologist, in a paper titled 'Childhood as a conversation of gestures' (1972) has called attention to the sort of mutual exchange of messages in extralinguistic modalities on which socialization depends.

It is my belief that interactive experience and exchange of messages in all communicative modalities is at the basis of language development. Communicative capacity is present in humans at birth and, under favorable circumstances, undergoes progressive elaboration and differentiation both before and after use of spoken language can be recognized.

The human infant emits both un-directed and directed messages. The un-directed, or 'to-whom-it-may-concern', message expresses his state at the time he produces it. In infancy most of such messages are usually classified as physiological. Such a message may or may not qualify as communication since it does not fit the customary paradigm of 'emitter-message-receiver' very neatly. I will not discuss this type of message here.

On the other hand, the directed message is produced in the context of an interaction, usually with a familiar, and it anticipates a response. The response need not be in the same modality as the message. For instance, one partner may indicate a desired object by directed gaze and the other may reply by proffering the object. In the case of directed messages the context for conversation is set up.

There are certain features of conversation, its more formal

characteristics, which even an infant can utilize in a way which does not require us to revise the concept of conversation beyond recognition. One which has been the subject of recent research is turn-taking (e.g., Duncan 1975, Markel 1975, Sacks et al. 1974). In addition, face-to-face conversation (as distinguished from, for instance, conversation by telephone) is usually characterized by mutual orientation of the participants involving not only posture but also patterned mutual gaze. These aspects have been described in detail for adults by Kendon (1973). Social language is probably involved since there is evidence that the details are culturally specific (e.g., Erickson 1975, Lomax 1975). Nor is it surprising to find infants exhibiting precursors of adult patterns of communicative interaction when they interact with adults, for adults cannot help but bring their established social skills to their transactions with infants, albeit in modified form. Infants are extraordinarily adaptive in their interactions with their adult familiars as shown, for instance, in their postural conforming on being handled.

Another characteristic of conversation is that it is usually about something. That something may be basically about the ongoing relationship that the conversation seeks to perpetuate, that is, phatic communication. But it may also, and usually does, involve reference to something outside the conversation itself. The early development of ways of making reference must contribute to the development of conversation.

I intend to present the results of two investigations involving directed messages in infancy and toddlerhood, each based on the work of a linguist at one time associated with me in my study of communicative development. Then I will report a little investigation of my own on some extralinguistic aspects of early communication. All of these studies have used as data longitudinal recordings on audio-tape and film of several normally developing middle-class Caucasian first-born infants who were observed weekly, from birth, in their own homes. I recorded these observations in the early 1960s. (For description of methodology, see Bullowa, Jones and Bever 1964). Since 1965 the tapes, films, transcripts and other documentation of these observations have been housed and studied at Massachusetts Institute of Technology.

One of these studies deals with phatic communication in

conversational mode long before the infant can contribute a recognizable language element. Another deals with the transition early in language development from present-time speaker-bound 'performative utterances' to a more advanced less constricted utterance type. In the more primitive utterance type an obligatory non-verbal component accompanied the child's speech, often clarifying the meaning. Finally I have traced this extralinguistic aspect of performative utterance back to its functionally equivalent precursors. All of these studies were based on observations of infants interacting with adults and usually in 'conversation' with them.

Proto-conversation
The first work I will describe was done by Mary Catherine Bateson, an anthropological linguist who was working with me from 1969 through 1971. During the time in which she was becoming familiar with the audio-tapes, from observations of the infants I had been following, she gave birth to her daughter and went through the first months of interaction with her. She began to realize that she was experiencing as a mother with her baby something she could recognize on the tapes: she was holding 'conversations' with this very young baby in which she and the baby were participating both vocally and in other ways. We matched the examples on the research tapes with their corresponding film passages and found a rather stereotyped sort of situation in which these exchanges took place. Mother and baby were facing each other at arms' length, appeared to be looking at each other and smiled and nodded frequently. Bateson called these exchanges 'proto-conversation'. Vocal interchanges may also occur when the mother is bathing, feeding, and doing other things to and for the baby. It would be more complicated to analyze the data from such 'instrumental' activities, and Bateson wanted to study these early conversation-like episodes in 'pure culture'. Her statistical analysis of some of this material was limited to situations in which no other activity was going on at the time.[1]

The following account of 'proto-conversation' starts with Bateson's first published report: 'Early in infancy, interactional sequences appear between mother and child which have the appearance of conversation: constant or nearly constant communication in one modality (visual) and intermittent, alternating communication in another (vocal)' (1971: 170). Bateson went on to refer to literature on the importance of eye-to-eye contact in early social development and experiments showing that infant non-cry vocalization could be increased by non-vocal social stimuli such as touch, visible presence, smiling, etc. using an operant conditioning paradigm. She pointed out that such studies ignore the interplay between mother and infant in which each affects the other's behavior. The intent of her method of study was to demonstrate in a statistically valid way the interactional aspect of the joint performances on which she was focussing her attention. This she stated as follows:

> The thrust of the present study is to describe the struc-
> ture of the interactions themselves, with special attention
> to the development of patterns of alternation in which
> contexts for speech may be constructed. Such an analysis
> depends on a concept of conversation that focuses
> primarily on the importance of vocal exchange in
> affirming contact (which Malinowski referred to as
> 'phatic communion'), rather than on content or the
> exchange of information. This orientation has been
> followed in a number of studies of adult communication.
> From this point of view, the 'protoconversations' of
> preverbal infants and their mothers can be treated as
> equivalent to the conversations of adults. The develop-
> ment of the capacity for participation in complex
> sequenced behavior must lay the groundwork for par-
> ticipation in games and for the development of linguistic
> performance; an ability to manipulate and recombine
> sequences may be significantly related to the develop-
> ment of linguistic competence. An understanding of
> interactional sequences may also be expected to lay
> important groundwork for better descriptions of imitative
> behavior. (ibid.: 171)

Examples of proto-conversation could be found by project-
ing films, originally taken at two frames per second, at faster
speeds and stopping when the suggestive spatial configuration
of mother and infant was noticed. Matching these passages
at normal (two per second) speed with the audio-tapes taken

simultaneously usually disclosed proto-conversations in progress. Examples that consisted of a number of turns were selected for study. The study was based on examples from one infant-mother pair from about two to about three and a half months of the infant's (Mackie's) age. This represents a small proportion of the instances found for this child. This type of interaction was found in the records of all of the five children for whom we have this sort of observational material. The tapes were put through a graphic level recorder to produce a pen and ink trace so that onset of each vocalization could be identified and its length (duration) could be measured.

Here is a description of the procedure and findings in Dr Bateson's words:

> The following criteria were used in selecting sequences: frequent vocalization by both mother and infant (excluding crying); generally sustained eye contact; and absence of caretaking activities that might have complicated the temporal pattern of vocalization. Sequences selected by these criteria showed several regularities. They tended to follow periods of active caretaking, and typically, mother and infant were less than a yard apart, with the mother's face frequently at the baby's level. On the other hand, there are occasions in the corpus in which the mother apparently tried to start a 'conversation', using the same postures and utterances, but without engaging the infant's attention, so that eye contact and responsive vocalization are absent. (1975: 102)

The apparently sustained eye contact is found to be actually intermittent when analyzed in greater detail. This has also been described by Stern (1971), who has done extensive studies on mother-infant gaze patterns with infants at around the same age. The gaze pattern in such pairs does differ from the fully developed adult to adult conversational gaze pattern described by Kendon (1973) in that in the adult situation the speaker meets the listener's gaze at the beginnings and ends of his utterances and the listener tends to watch the speaker throughout. The speaker's gaze behavior appears to contain messages about his intention to continue speaking or to yield the floor. This does not apply in adult to infant speech.

Kendon recognized the need for studies of gaze behavior in kinds of encounters other than those he has analyzed (ibid.: 62). The conversational situation that Bateson described may have more in common with communication between lovers than with that between the strangers and mere acquaintances analyzed by Kendon.

As in Kendon's analysis of dyadic conversations, each maintains body orientation toward the other despite occasional brief looks away. The mother may or may not be supporting the infant. Body contact is not essential but is not precluded during this activity.

What Bateson wanted to find out was whether the mother's and infant's vocalizations were influencing the other partner, since, if so, this would support the idea that this activity foreshadows conversation. It is conceivable that two individuals could vocalize or speak in one another's presence without their vocalization being responsive, for instance if one or both were deaf.

This is how Bateson analyzed the data and what she found in her own words:

> The overall effect of alternating vocalization and the degree to which alternation of the two parties deviated from the random were computed by pooling the number of runs of particular lengths by each speaker and comparing the observed frequencies of each length with expected frequency, by chi-square test. (1975: 104)

The findings demonstrated that the mother and infant vocalized by turns. She then turned to analyzing the timing of the vocalization. Continuing to quote:

> Thus, when we examine a hypothesis of the mother inserting vocalizations in a stream of random vocalizations by the infant in terms of timing, we find that the mean time between onsets of all infant vocalizations in this sample, regardless of maternal vocalization, is 3.14 sec (s=4.27); on the other hand, this hypothesis could be reversed, with the infant simply inserting vocalizations. The mean onset to onset time for the mother is 2.96 (s=2.24) which is not significantly different from the timing of the infant. (1975: 104)

Bateson then looked at evidence that some utterances in

a sequence were responsive and some appeared to have the intent of renewing a lagging exchange.

> For both mother and infant, the mean time of utterance onset from onset of previous utterance is longer when the previous utterance was by self than when previous utterance was by other . . . In effect, the time from onset of utterance by other to own onset may be characterized as *response* time, whereas the time from onset of self to repeated onset by self may be characterized as *elicitation* time; apparently the mother says something (often a question) and waits for a response from the infant before renewing her vocalization. The difference is significant at the 0.01 level for the mother. Although it is not significant for the infant, the tendency is in the same direction, with all interval types somewhat briefer for the infant. It is also notable that mother and child rarely interrupt one another. (1975: 105)

Dr Bateson felt that she had not only described a very common phenomenon of infancy but had shown that the vocalization of one partner made a difference in the subsequent vocalization of the other by speeding its onset.

There is in the literature a statement that appears to question the concept that early conversation-like behavior prefigures adult conversation. Jaffe, Stern and Peery (1973), without referring to Bateson's first report, question the relevance to verbal conversational patterns of a phenomenon that they characterize as 'conversational' coupling of gaze behavior in prelinguistic human development. Their study compared gazing patterns of infant-adult dyads with temporal patterns of adult *spoken* conversation. The statement in question reads: 'We do not consider the "conversational" coupling of early gazing behavior to be a precursor of verbal conversational patterns – it is rather, more obviously, a precursor of later gazing patterns. However, both are communicative systems whose maturation requires coordination with the other. Our central point is that the common mathematical regularity may represent some universal formal property of dyadic communication which is detectable in infant gazing behavior long before the onset of speech.' (p.327)

In January of 1975 Dr Bateson participated in a symposium

on 'Developmental Psycholinguistics and Communication Disorders' at the New York Academy of Sciences. There she presented the substance of her study on proto-conversation in amplified form. Daniel N. Stern, one of the co-authors of the paper that had seemed to disagree with Bateson's interpretation, participated too and, fortunately, subsequent discussion of the issue in which both of them and others took part has been published, so that the apparent disagreement could be resolved.

Jaffe, Stern and Peery (1973) had been considering both gaze behavior and vocalization in mother-infant dydads in terms of states ('on' or 'off' in either modality). Either, both, or neither might be looking at the other's face in any of the 0.6 sec. intervals coded. Vocalization was likewise considered as having two states: vocalizing or pausing. For each system (gazing and vocalizing) only four joint configurations of mother and infant could occur. The analysis consisted of computing transition matrices from state to state. 'A Markov chain structure is discovered for both systems such that the probability of entering any dyadic state usually depends on a history of less than a second . . . Discovery of a Markovian structure, so ubiquitous in nature, as common to the two systems might be merely a mathematical curiosity were it not for the fact that these systems are so intimately coordinated in normal conversation.' (p.327 just preceding quotation above). It should be noted that the paper, 'Vocalizing in unison and in alternation: two modes of communication within the mother-infant dyad' by Stern, Jaffe, Beebe and Bennett which was under discussion at the 1975 conference dealt with a different theme. However, the issue was the same except that by now mother-infant vocal co-action, contrasted with vocal alternation, was also considered. They had studied vocalization in play sessions between mothers and their three- to four-month-old infants and had found both alternation and co-action with co-action much the more frequent. They contended that these two patterns serve different purposes and have different developments. They considered the alternating mode, the more 'adult' one and predicted that it would become more prominent with the development of speech, whereas they considered the coactional pattern to be associated with infancy and states of 'high arousal'.

In reply to a comment from the audience to the effect that Bateson's kids know so much more about alternation than Stern's, Bateson responded: 'Yes, but our sampling of situations was very different. I selected the pieces I looked at out of the data because I was interested in alternation, and I was working with one mother-child pair; so there's nothing in my data that says anything about the frequency of co-action' (in Aaronson and Rieber 1975: 165). In response to a comment about the isolation of modalities, Bateson responded: '. . . when you open it up to all the modalities, you virtually have to say that in most of these interactions there's co-action throughout. The real question is: do we sometimes take turns in one or more modalities as an ongoing interaction?' (ibid.: 164) Stern replied:

> That is very well put and changes, in part, the ball park in which we talk about interactions. We frequently see the kind of interaction where the mother may voke [vocalize] and the baby responds by turning away or by turning away with a smile, whereupon the mother says something else, and the baby may toss his head up and open his mouth, or voke, and then the mother says something again and the baby this time responds by returning his gaze to her, and so on. She reacts to each infant behavior as if it were a verbal response following the adult discursive model. Similarly, you see many mothers who are terrific with their tactile behavior (I'm sure you've seen this), so that they can keep the ball going, so to speak, by putting the touching or jiggling in at the right places. I quite agree with you; it requires a reconceptualization of what we're talking about (ibid.: 164-5)

So, in considering 'conversation' patterns in infant-adult communication, we've come in less than five years from talking about vocalization eliciting vocalization and gaze eliciting gaze to considering many more ways in which people, infants included, can demonstrate their mutual responsiveness. Conversation, as I think both Professor Halliday and Professor Lyons would agree, is not an entirely linguistic matter.

The age of two months does not represent the onset of this infant-caregiver behavior. I have had the opportunity to make frequent observations beginning as soon after birth as feasible in an American and in a British family. I found each of these mother-infant pairs engaging in face-to-face 'conversation' from as early as I was able to get to the hospitals to observe them. In one instance the baby was a few hours, in the other a few days old. It seems to be a spontaneous behavior of mothers in our culture to initiate such behavior and for infants when awake and in the appropriate position vis-à-vis the mother, to gaze at her face and vocalize softly. Such early exchanges are usually very brief.

Recent interest in providing opportunities for mothers to have access to their newborn infants in the interest of facilitating emotional bonding led to research which showed that mothers, given the chance, will position the newborns *en face* and seek contact by touch, gaze and voice (Klaus et al 1970).

Condon and Sander (1974) have demonstrated the differential response of newborns to human voice in contrast to all other sounds. This consists in synchronization of body movement with the fine structure of the attended speech. Synchronization is tuned to the shift from one phone to the next. This is a phenomenon that cannot be discerned with the naked eye since it occurs at a frequency of the order of ten times per second. It is not necessary for eye contact to accompany the infant's auditory attention, since the phenomenon has been demonstrated with recorded voice. Nor does the voice need to be that of the mother. What this important research finding emphasizes is the fine tuning to human speech that the human infant possesses at birth. Condon and Sander were analyzing only adult speech and infant movement so we do not know whether infant vocalization occurred. Eisenberg (1975: 384) in non-interactive testing has demonstrated differential neonatal response to speech and non-speech auditory stimuli.

Performatives

I will now present a considerably later aspect of communicative development investigated by Jeffrey S. Gruber using tape from the same data collection. Dr Gruber is an M.I.T.-trained linguist who has developed and written within a theory of lexically oriented generative semantics. His studies on child language were done from 1965 to 1967 and these findings were presented at a meeting of the Society for Research in Child Development in 1967.[2] Gruber was working in the M.I.T. linguistic context and at the time when John Ross (of M.I.T.) was first advocating the concept of the performative in the base structure of language (1970). This stemmed from Austin's proposal about performatives propounded in his book: *How to Do Things with Words* (1962).

Gruber studied the early utterances of a child (Dory) starting from when he could recognize that she was making novel combinations at least two words in length.[3] He excluded repetitions immediately after the mother and 'set phrases' from his corpus of child utterances. (The corpus is published with the paper.) On the basis of linguistic analysis he came to the conclusion that the first novel utterances were overt performatives only — that is that they expressed what the child was in fact doing by means of his utterance.[4] The two types that were predominant at this time were 'indication',[5] such as 'see kitty' and 'request', such as 'wanna cookie'. He worked this out without reference to the film. (In fact, when he did the original analysis we were not able to put tape and film together in synchrony.) He found that, beginning with the first appearance of two-word utterances at 15 months, for nine consecutive weeks all of Dory's utterances could be classified as performative sentences. In many of these sentences a verb form did not express the performative, but rather the name of the speaker or the person addressed was used to do so. There were a number of alternative combinations of word types, but all of them, he felt, represented sentences of the performative type. In the tenth week, at 17½ months, the child began, by embedding into performative sentences, to produce sentences, which he called at the time 'reportative'. (in the later version, 'constative'). Very often the performative sentences did not appear in the surface structure of this more advanced type of sentence with which the child could talk about things not directly tied to her utterance. For example, she could use as subject someone or something other than herself or the addressee.

After he had distinguished these sentence types, and in preparation for the presentation at the SRCD meeting, we were fortunate in having equipment available that made it possible to synchronize tape and film. It then became apparent that every time the child was heard on tape to utter one of the sentences that Gruber had identified as performative, she was seen to perform the corresponding action on the screen. Gruber (1973: 443) drew the conclusion in this paper that: 'Both the speech and the accompanying bodily activity represent the same communicative act. The speech act is for the child indistinguishable from the act of reaching for the object.'

It is noteworthy that most of Dory's performative utterances involved an object or action that she was requesting or at least calling to attention. That is, even though these utterances were closely bound to Dory's immediate state, at the same time they made reference beyond the I-thou of the communicating dyad. This is no longer purely phatic communication, even though it may include or imply a phatic element.

Deictic Development

In the fall of 1973 Gruber was about to submit a revision of his paper for publication and sent me a copy of the manuscript. I went back to the original data to check it and then it occurred to me that, not only did the verbal aspect of these communications have a development, but also the behavioral aspect must develop too. I started by identifying the forms of behavior that coincided with Gruber's corpus of performatives: the 'see' and 'wanna' utterances. At 15 months the pointing to indicate and the reaching for desired objects seemed distinct. Either might be and often was accompanied by bodily movement in the same direction. But, as I traced the behaviors backward month by month, the distinction between pointing and reaching behavior became less marked. Werner and Kaplan (1963), in a chapter on 'Precursors and early stages of denotative reference' challenge the contention that pointing derives from grasping, but also acknowledge that '. . . there seems to be some element of reference in the bodily acts of reaching' (p.78). Whether or not reaching and pointing have separate origins, in terms of the temporal sequence of the appearance of deictic behaviors, reaching as a recognizable gesture does precede pointing.

In my backward-ordered descriptions, starting from the behavioral precursors of the complete verbal-behavioral performatives of the Gruber corpus, pointing seemed to drop out. It is possible that at the period of the Gruber corpus (15 to 17½ months) pointing had been associated with naming. Earlier the purpose of indication had seemed to focus on demand for an object, for contact, for attention, etc. It was also apparent that gaze behavior usually accompanied hand behavior. The gaze could be toward what was wanted or toward the person of whom it was wanted if these were in different directions. Often there was no need to choose. Still earlier, around three months, Dory tended to indicate what she wanted by gaze alone. Indication of what is requested is implied in request behavior, whatever form it takes.

Directed gaze as a gesture to focus on something specific, although it starts very early in life, is not replaced by hand-arm gestures. Rather these gestures are added to the repertoire as reaching, grasping, pointing, etc. become differentiated and voluntarily controlled. In Kendon's studies of behavior in relation to talk in adult life, gaze is an important aspect, as it is in most of human social behavior. Since gaze is the most mature motor function at birth, it is not surprising that gaze had a prominent place both in identifying Bateson's proto-conversations and in my survey of what might be called 'proto-deictic' behavior.

An infant at first is not able to free himself from the bilaterality of his movements when in symmetrical positions. When his head is oriented straight ahead so that he can look, he can't reach unless he is in an appropriate tilted position with his head higher than his feet as pointed out by Bower (1972) of Edinburgh University, and then he reaches with both hands. The importance of gaze behavior as indicating what the child is interested in has been very well illustrated by Collis and Schaffer (1975), who have studied the way in which maternal gaze lines up with her infant's gaze very early, even when they are facing in the same direction so that she cannot see his face.

It occurred to me that the coincidence of gaze and hand-extending behavior in the early months could be related to the tonic neck reflex in which turning an infant's head to one side produces extension of the arm on the side to which the head faces. I found that Gesell, who had made detailed investigations of the development of posture and locomotion and had emphasized the role of the tonic neck reflex in this development, had written a book (1949) on the development of visual behavior in which he demonstrated the relationship I had surmised.

After tracing Dory's directed attentive behavior backward to the gaze-only stage at the end of her third month of life, (as early as I was able to trace it in the films I had of her), I scanned the series of films of Mackie, Bateson's subject. I started with observations at one month and traced his directed behaviors forward until they linked up with speech. In both series the maternal responses were usually expressed in action with or without words. But it was clear that these two mothers understood the requesting and indicating behaviors of their babies from the start, whether or not they complied. For instance, Mackie's mother while holding him on her lap for dressing (when he was eight months old) picked up a dropped object a number of times and finally continued with the dressing when he dropped it again and appealed to her to retrieve it by leaning over and reaching toward it. She did not disregard the request but indicated that he would have to wait. I was nearby and had a free hand. When Mackie turned his appeal to me by gaze, I could not resist it and retrieved it for him. This was well before he could name the object (shoe) in a way that would have qualified as speech. In scanning the Mackie observations going forward after having scanned the Dory ones backward, I found the same sequence: gaze, reach, point and speak.[6]

So one might say babies first converse with their eyes, then bring in their hands and finally add spoken language. In this way they assemble the complex of communicative modalities which Kendon has described for adult conversation (op. cit.). Kendon's analysis deals also with spacing, posture and body orientation as well as with movement patterns and he has included movements other than those of head, eyes and hands, none of which I have yet studied in infant-adult conversation. He points out that when adults engage in conversation 'they organize their behavior into certain units of communicative behavior which follow one another in a set of patterned relationships irrespective of the topics discussed' (p.68). These behaviors have as much to be 'acquired' as the linguistic component of conversation. If one looks closely at what babies do in their transactions with adults, one can see them starting to adopt conversational behaviors long before one can understand their vocalizations as speech.

Conclusion

What I have been trying to convey to you by means of a few examples is that human babies, given half a chance, can be good company — good conversational partners to their adult caregivers, especially to their mothers. In the 'conversation of gestures' the baby is at first often making demands, but he is also capable of entering into a more disinterested kind of communication in which each partner expresses sheer delight in the other's company. As his capacities unfold, he adds and elaborates new ways to communicate his needs and wishes well in advance of his capacity to use speech. Nevertheless, at the same time he is already well on his way to discovering vocal devices for differentiating meanings, as Halliday (this Symposium) has demonstrated.

The earliest extra-uterine communication, the kind which Klaus and Kennell and others have documented, when mothers are given access to their newborns in defiance of long established hospital practice, is entirely about itself — about the relationship between the I and thou who so recently seemed to have been one. But very soon the baby expresses his ability to communicate about something in addition and so deixis enters the picture. Whether or not reaching and pointing have separate behavioral antecedents, both share the function of specifying a particular something and, unless what is referred to is all or part of the self, this necessarily introduces a third term into the conversation: it now concerns some specified person or thing or action, even though the specification is achieved by extra-linguistic means. As the child enters his language community he elaborates this specification still further. Once he could refer to only what was immediately present with him and his partner at the time. Now he can, through the use of language, make reference to things, persons, events at a distance in time and space and so extend his conversational capability.[7]

Notes

1.   At this point in the presentation I showed a portion of video tape recorded in the research playroom of N. Blurton Jones' laboratory of human ethology at the Institute of Child Health, University of London, because I did not have access to film from my own collection. Since the activity is widespread in transactions between infants and their caregiving adults, at least in Anglo-American middle-class culture, it was reasonable to expect to find examples in any video-tape or film of infants and caregiving adults whose activity was directed by the investigator. The Blurton Jones tapes, which were taken for another purpose, focussed on the older siblings of the infants whom I discovered on the tapes so that the proto-conversations I found were recorded almost by accident. The segment selected for demonstration showed characteristic vis-à-vis positioning of mother and infant, even though the infant was on his back in a playpen and the mother was leaning over in order to communicate with him. Since the mothers in the playroom situation were focussed on their older children, most of the other examples I had found were embedded in caregiving activity.

2.   The original version was published in Ferguson and Slobin's 'Studies of Child Language Development'. A revised version has since been published in *Foundations of Language*.

3.   'Dory' was a precocious child whose language use started before she was ten months old (cf. 'The acquisition of a word', in Bullowa, Jones and Duckert, *Language and Speech* (1964) vol. 7 pt. 2, 107-11.

4.   A performative doesn't merely express what one is doing *while* one speaks, but rather *by* one's speech act. Saying 'I demand (request) the cookie' is the demand itself; 'I indicate the kitty' is the indication itself: equal to reaching and pointing as communicative acts.

5.   'Indicate' and 'indication' are the terms Gruber used in his original formulation in 1967 and continued to use in his revision. Although he seems not to distinguish between behavioral and linguistic uses of these terms, it is my impression that, as a linguist, he intended a strict linguistic usage. Gruber read an earlier version of this paper and requested that I retain the term 'indicate'.

6.   Many years ago, when I was about to start to study the ontogeny of communication, I went to see Professor Heinz Werner, by then in retirement. He graciously advised me how to undertake my studies. The piece of advice that remained prominent in my recollection of my visit to that 'grand old man' of child development was that if you want to find the earliest *anlage* of a behavior you should start from where it is well established and work back-

ward through your data. I doubt that he intended me to trace a function rather than a behavior in this way, but that was how I applied his advice in this instance.

7.   The studies on which this paper is based were done in the laboratory of the Speech Communication group, Research Laboratory of Electronics, Massachusetts Institute of Technology, Director, Professor Kenneth N. Stevens, under N I H grant No. NS 04332. The paper was prepared for presentation while I was a guest of the laboratory of Dr N. Blurton Jones in the Department of Growth and Development (Professor John Tanner, Director), at the Institute of Child Health, University of London. I want to express my gratitude to both institutions for their hospitality.

Acknowledgement
I would like to thank the New York Academy of Sciences for permission to quote from D. Aaronson and W. Rieber (eds) *Developmental Psycholinguistics and Communication Disorders* (1975).

RULES AND PROCEDURES IN DISCOURSE ANALYSIS

I want to use this occasion to try to set my thoughts in order. What I should like to do is to work out my own tentative methodological bearings on the area of enquiry that goes under the general name of discourse analysis. I do not wish to claim that this is anything but an exercise in clarification for myself and my only justification for thinking aloud in public is that some of the issues that trouble me may be troublesome for other people as well.

It seems to me (to begin on a general, reflective note) that the central issue in discourse analysis relates to the old problem of distinguishing between what people know and what people do. It has been generally assumed that the essential facts regarding what people do with their language can be accounted for by rules describing their knowledge, that performance is a projection of competence. The proposing of an extended notion of competence to embrace a knowledge of how linguistic forms are used in the performance of appropriate communicative acts has not essentially altered the basic assumption that knowledge in some sense *determines* behaviour. It is still generally held that communicative activity is rule-*governed*, with the implication that once the rules are specified we automatically account for how people use language.

But in what sense do rules *determine* behaviour, and how do they *govern* our actions? The fact that there is considerable room for manoeuvre in individuals makes it clear that there are no absolute constraints upon us. A good deal of what we do, linguistically and otherwise, seems not to conform exactly to rules, seems indeed to be a manipulation of rules to suit particular occasions. Now, is this individual variation, this freedom of speech, so random as to be beyond the scope of systematic enquiry? If not, there would appear to be two possibilities:

either the rules for knowledge that have been specified are not yet at least sufficiently refined to capture these aspects of use, although in principle they can be so refined; or we need to formulate statements about behaviour that are not expressed in the form of rules, or at least not in the form of the same kind of rules as are used to account for knowledge.

I do not think that it is possible to account for how people behave simply by specifying rules for knowledge, whether these relate to linguistic or communicative competence. It seems to me that if one attempts to do so, one gets into all kinds of difficulties. How, for example, do we explain stylistic innovation and our ability to interpret its meaning and appreciate its effect? There has been a tendency among some generative grammarians to dismiss such phenomena as metaphor, for instance, as somewhat aberrant ways of using language, and of course it may be convenient to take this view when constructing a sentence grammar. But metaphor surely lies at the heart of our everyday communicative behaviour. What seems to be abnormal is *non*-metaphorical communication, a strict conformity to rule. Indeed if language users were strict conformists their language would presumably lose its capacity for adaptation and would gradually fossilise.

Now of course innovatory uses of language are understood *in relation* to our knowledge of rules. But how do we bring these rules to bear? How do we use them in the production and interpretation of instances of communicative behaviour? It cannot simply be a matter of correlation: we do not just *identify* instances of use as manifesting the rules we already know. We draw upon our knowledge of rules to *make sense*. We do not simply measure discourse up against our knowledge of pre-existing rules, we create discourse and commonly bring new rules into existence by so doing. All competence is transitional in this sense. Knowledge and behaviour are interdependent; what we do is to some degree relatable to what we know, but what we do also extends the scope of our knowledge. This, I take it, is what learning means. It seems to me that the central task in discourse analysis must be the investigation of this interrelationship.

So I want to suggest a distinction between *rules*, which represent what we know and to which we make reference when we use language, and the *procedures* we employ in realising the communicative import of language in use. I suppose one might call these procedures 'rules of performance' but this term 'performance' is not free of the taint of dogma and its use here might suggest, first, that these rules are of less immediate concern than those relating to knowledge — competence rules — and secondly that they are dependent upon them unilaterally, that the competence rules 'underlie' performance rules. But I want to suggest that both kinds of 'rule' have a claim on our concern and that one kind does not have any natural precedence over the other. I also feel that the notion of rule loses precision when it is applied both to a pre-existing principle and to the manner in which we refer to it in actual behaviour. So I think we might find it useful to make a terminological distinction between rule and procedure.

Let me follow established tradition at this point by illustrating the distinction I am trying to make by reference to the game of chess. We may claim that we know how to play the game if we know the moves it is permitted to make with different pieces, that is to say, if we know the constitutive rules of the game. But when we are actually engaging an opponent, we do not merely move our pieces in accordance with these rules: we *use* these rules to create openings, to develop a plan of campaign, to make a game of it. Although the moves we make do, of course, manifest rules and can be referred to as evidence that we know how to play (that we know that the different pieces can only be moved in certain specific pre-ordained ways), what is of interest to the players (and the observers of the game) is the manner in which these rules are being manipulated, the procedures whereby each player tries to get into a favourable position and which demonstrate his skill in using his knowledge of the rules. At any point in the game each player is faced with a number of possibilities, created by his own manoeuvres as limited by the manoeuvres of his opponent, and he chooses one of the possibilities, anticipating his opponent's move and of course shifting the whole pattern of the game at the same time. As I shall suggest presently, it is very like conversation. Now certain procedures may in the course of time take on the status of rules. I know nothing about the history of chess, nor of the conventions that are held to constitute acceptable chess behaviour in particular groups of players, but I would suppose that as certain procedures become common practice they assume the role of rules and are considered to be constitutive of the game. So I should think it likely that there is change and variation in chess just as there is change and variation in langugage and that in both cases they proceed from particular ways of using the existing rules.

I want now to make a distinction between two kinds of rule. The first kind, which I will refer to as rules of usage, account for linguistic competence in the Chomskyan sense: they represent the language user's knowledge of the formal systems of his language. We might say that they constitute his basic grammatical source of reference. The second, which I will refer to as rules of use, account for the language user's knowledge of speech acts and can be said to constitute his basic communicative source of reference. The kind of enquiry conducted in Austin (1962) and Searle (1969), for example, is directed towards a formulation of rules of use. Such rules relate to our knowledge of what it is to promise, warn, predict, insult and so on, of what certain activities, not necessarily linguistic, conventionally count as.

Both rules of usage and rules of use are subject to variation. Chomsky and Searle deal in ideal cases: sentences and acts in standardised abstraction. But just as there are different kinds of usage operating in dialects, so there are different kinds of use operating in different universes of discourse. For example, we may know what it is to explain something and what constitutes agreement within the conventions accepted within our particular areas of social operation, but it does not follow that we know what counts as a scientific explanation or a legal agreement. Problems arise when we attempt to transfer rules of use from one universe-of-discourse to another. I take it that one of the central concerns of formal education is to resolve this problem and to extend the repertoire of such rules.

One of the central concerns in linguistic description, on the other hand, is the specification of the relationship between these two kinds of rule. Can we, for example, incorporate illocutions into grammar by means of a super-ordinate performative sentence as is proposed in Ross (1970)? Can we not simply deal with speech act analysis in terms of the semantic analysis of performative verbs, as is proposed in Fillmore (1971)? What is the relationship between the semantics of performative verbs recorded in a lexicon and accounted for, therefore, as usage, and the pragmatics of actual communication which attempts to account for the acts that these verbs are customarily used to refer to, and which has therefore to do with use? Is the knowledge of what a verb like *promise* means the same as knowing how to promise as a social activity? Questions like these appear against a background of old issues like the relationship between sign and concept, and between language, thought and behaviour.

And questions like these are sometimes confused with questions of another kind: those that relate to the link between rules and procedures. Questions concerning the relationship between different kinds of rule (whether, for example, illocutions can be accommodated in the base component of a generative grammar) are different from (though ultimately related to) questions concerning the manner in which particular acts are realised in particular circumstances.

How the uttering of a certain linguistic form comes to take on the illocutionary force of a promise, request, explanation, or what have you, has to do with the procedure of making sense. Rules of use are one thing, but *procedures* of use are another. Let us consider an example. Labov proposes a number of what he calls 'pre-conditions' for the performance of the act of ordering or requesting action. The specification of such pre-conditions is in effect, like Searle's characterisation of different speech acts, a formulation of rules of use. But Labov then goes on to demonstrate how these rules are deployed in actual behaviour, how speakers put their knowledge to work in creating coherent discourse. Thus, having defined the act of ordering in terms of four necessary pre-conditions, he then describes what I would wish to call a procedure whereby a particular utterance is taken as counting as this particular act. He expresses this procedure as follows:

> If A makes a request for information of B about whether
> an action X has been performed, or at what time, T, X

will be performed, and the four pre-conditions hold,
then A will be heard as making a request for action.
(Labov 1972: 256)

It will be noted that it is taken for granted that a request
for information will be recognised as self-evident here, but of
course one will need to describe the procedure whereby
this act is realised in discourse by reference to *its* rules. In the
paper referred to above, Labov leaves one with the impression
that he does not see the relationship between rules and procedures as particularly problematic. This is not the impression
one gets from the work of the ethnomethodologists.

In a well-known paper, Sacks, for example, investigates
what it is that enables us to hear the two utterances 'The baby
cried. The mummy picked it up' as a complete and coherent
narrative (Sacks 1972). His investigation makes reference to
what he calls 'membership categorisation devices'. These
consist of collections of membership categories and application
rules. The former would appear to be semantic constructs
and to be, therefore, Sacks' somewhat idiosyncratic expression
of rules of usage. His application rules, on the other hand,
refer to the manner in which the language user's knowledge
of such devices is used to make sense of the particular instance
of discourse he is concerned with. One of these application
rules runs as follows:

> If some population of persons is being categorised, and
> if a category from some device's collection has been used
> to categorise a first member of the population, then that
> category, or other categories of the same collection *may*
> be used to categorise further members of the population.

A corollary to this 'rule' is what Sacks calls a 'hearer's
maxim', which runs as follows:

> If two or more categories are used to categorise two or
> more members of some population, and those categories
> can be heard as categories from the same collection, then:
> hear them that way. (Sacks 1972: 333)

There are a number of features in Sacks' description which
I find a little obscure, but it seems to me that what he is trying
to capture are the procedures that language users employ when
they make communicative sense of language data, the manner
in which they *use* their knowledge of semantics, or, as Sacks

would have it, membership categorisation devices as encoded in their language.

Both Labov and Sacks are concerned with the way a pair of actual utterances are recognised as being meaningfully related. In the case of Labov, the focus of attention is on the relationship between procedures and what I have called rules of use; and in the case of Sacks, the focus of attention is on the relationship between procedures and what I have called rules of usage. Following on from this observation, I want now to suggest that in discourse analysis we are concerned with procedures of two sorts: those that relate to rules of usage and that realise propositional development, which I will call *cohesion procedures*, and those that relate to rules of use and that realise the illocutionary development of discourse, which I will call *coherence procedures*.

By cohesion procedures I mean the way the language user traces propositional development in discourse by, for example, realising the appropriate value of anaphoric elements, the way in which a sequence of units of information encapsulated in linguistic units is provided with a conceptual unity. The devices of thematisation (cf. Halliday 1967/68, 1973) and grammatical cohesion (cf. Hasan 1968) can be described by rules of usage, just as can Sacks' categorisation devices, but how these devices are actually put to use on particular occasions is a matter of procedure. How, for example, do we select the appropriate value for a pronoun when there is more than one grammatically possible referential link? At what point is it necessary to relexicalise a reference? When does a discourse take on a life of its own so that the cumulative effect of what has preceded in some way takes precedence over individual meanings? When do the expectations created by the propositional development within a particular instance of discourse over-ride the meanings of particular propositions? To put it another way, when does the unity of the whole cease to depend on the separate significance of the parts? Questions like these have to do with the procedures whereby language users draw upon their knowledge of rules to synthesise meaning in discourse.

By coherence procedures I mean the way in which the language user realises what communicative act is being performed in the expression of particular propositions, and how different acts are related to each other in linear and hierarchical arrangements. Thus the recognition that a particular expression counts as an invitation rather than an order is a matter of realising that the context provides for the fulfilment of one set of conditions rather than another. Again, the adjustment of interpretation in the light of new evidence is also a matter of coherence procedure. I may, for example, interpret a particular remark as a casual observation and then be obliged to revise this interpretation as the discourse proceeds and as it becomes apparent that the remark was intended as, let us say, an explanation.

But coherence is not, I think, simply a matter of illocutionary connections in dissociation from propositional development. Procedures of cohesion and coherence are not entirely distinct, any more than are rules of usage and use. I think that there are two ways of looking at the communicative activity that goes on in the creation of discourse coherence. We can, on the one hand, consider a particular instance of discourse as a large scale illocutionary act of the Searlean sort and establish what constituent acts there are within it, these acts in effect realising the set of conditions that define the large scale act. Thus, we might wish to characterise a particular instance of discourse as a report consisting of such constituent acts as definition, hypothesis, description and so on. This kind of description focuses on the communicative intent of the speaker/writer in so far as it relates to the illocutionary acts he wishes to perform. In this view, propositions are only of interest to the extent that they serve to realise conditions on different acts. A second kind of approach would focus not so much on *what* communication is achieved in a discourse as on *how* the communication is achieved. Attention here is directed at the interaction management aspects of use. In this approach, different communicative acts are defined internally, as it were, with reference to their function as elements of discourse structure. Examples of such 'interactive'* acts would be agreement, disagreement, initiative, response, elicitation and most of the communicative units described in Sinclair and Coulthard (1975). With acts of this kind,

* I owe the use of this term to my colleague Hugh Trappes-Lomax.

the proposition does not simply enter into the picture as a
condition but is central to the act itself. We might say, in
fact, that in the case of illocutionary acts of the Searlean
kind the proposition is ancillary to the act, whereas in the case
of these interactive acts the act is ancillary to the proposition.

We might regard interactive acts, then, as instruments of
propositional development. In this respect they serve as the
link between cohesion and coherence procedures. But now the
question might arise: how can interactive procedures operate
when there is no interaction, as would appear to be the case
in written discourse? This question touches on the relationship
between production and interpretation. It seems to me that all
discourse is interactive and that the same interpretation
procedures are brought into play whether one is involved in
the actual production of discourse or not. When a spoken
interaction takes place each participant develops his own
scheme, which he adjusts according to what his interlocutor
says. I am sure that it is a mistake to suppose that one participant's responses are simply reactions to what the other has
said: they are, rather, readjustments to his own communicative
intents. As I have already suggested, verbal interactions resemble
games of chess: each participant works out his moves in
advance and modifies them tactically as the encounter develops.
In a serious game, analogous to academic argument, each
player will be trying to project his own pattern on the game
and to force his opponent into error, or at least into a move
that can be turned to advantage. The producer of written
discourse is playing with an unseen, and often, to some degree
at least, an unknown player, although he will usually have a
fair idea of what skill to allow for and will play the game
accordingly. In the case of written discourse, the player/
producer anticipates his opponent's moves by writing them
into the discourse. In consequence, the game may well proceed
in a way that is different from the way the writer originally
intended it to go because his anticipation modifies his intentions.
And the reader too begins to anticipate from the first move
onwards, and plays his own game as he reads. When we talk
of monologue and dialogue we refer to the overt differences
of surface performance, but it seems likely that the same
interactive interpretation process underlies both.

Let me now draw a simple sketch map of what I have been trying to work out. We have rules of usage and rules of use and these together constitute what a language user knows. The relationship between them is problematic but a likely link is modality. We have procedures that represent what a language user does with his knowledge in the creation, productively or receptively, of discourse that has propositional cohesion and illocutionary coherence. A possible link between these is inter-activity. Interactivity, then, mediates between the procedures of cohesion and coherence in much the same way as modality mediates between the rules of usage and the rules of use. We might express these relationships as follows:

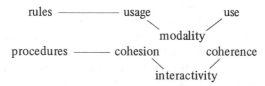

There is a deceptive neatness about this, an enchanting simplicity which distance lends to the view. But there are, of course, all kinds of difficulties that do not disappear simply by having a frame put around them. A major one has to do with orientation. In what I have said so far, for example, I have assumed that rules and procedures can be inferred from an observation of data; that the methodology of discourse analysis is in this respect straightforward. But it is really not straightforward at all because what the analyst observes is not necessarily what the participant experiences. This is the problem of ethnocentric contamination, which social anthropologists have been long aware of, as have researchers into child language acquisition, itself a kind of special branch of social anthropology. It is the same problem that has particularly exercised the minds of scholars working within ethnomethodology. It underlies the conflicts between stylistic analysis and literary criticism.

To put the matter simply, there are two possible methodological perspectives on discourse analysis. One can, on the one hand, deal with instances of discourse from the point of view of the third person analyst: that is to say, one can treat discourse in detachment from its instantiation, after the event, as a product. On the other hand, one can deal with discourse from the point of view of the participants caught, as it were, in the act; that is to say, one can treat discourse as a process. To return once more to our game of chess. At the end of a particular game, one can specify the moves that have been made and thereby give an account of the structure of that particular encounter. But this account does not of course record how the game developed from the player's point of view, it does not reveal the experience of planning moves, modifying them to counter the moves of the opponent and so on. A product analysis does not capture how the game assumed the structure it did assume, the process of the game's development.

I am not at all sure myself how far process analysis is possible. The ethnomethodologists seem to make claims that they are dealing with process, with the ongoing accomplishment of practical reasoning, but although they make inferences about process, they typically deal with products. There is no evidence, to my knowledge, that they have attempted to conduct experiments that might yield information about how the participants see the discourse at a particular point in its development and what controls their choice of options at this point. A process analysis should presumably take an interest not only in the paths that are taken but in those that are not but could have been.

In fact, I think there is a general and natural tendency for the analyst to withdraw from involvement, to come to terms with his data by putting himself at a distance from it and so reducing it in perspective to methodological size. The analyst is inclined to move from process to product, and then to convert procedures inferred from product into rules of use and then, wherever possible, into rules of usage. There is a comfortable sense of security to be found in the specification of precise invariant rules and we shall perhaps never feel really at our ease until we can express all behaviour as knowledge within a unitary theory of linguistic description; until all the creative procedures of human beings are expressed in terms of exact rules. But one sometimes wonders whether this sense of security is worth the price that one might be paying for it.

DEVELOPMENT OF TEXTURE IN CHILD LANGUAGE

I shall take it, then, following Margaret Bullowa's observations, that the capacity to communicate is present in humans from birth. That is to say, a child is born genetically endowed with the ability to take part in acts of communication; in Malcolm France's terms, he is sensitive to the phenomenon of address. He is aware of being addressed — he knows when he is being communicated with — and is predisposed to address others. Towards the end of his paper, Henry Widdowson made the remark that all discourse is in fact interaction; and if we combine these two lines of thought, we are faced with the question what steps the child must take in order to develop from being a potential communicator, a potential with which he is endowed by virtue of his humanity, to being one who takes part in the interactive processes of discourse. Our focus is therefore on the ability to construct text; I shall try to identify certain critical steps in the development of a mastery of texture, using as source material my own account of the language development of one child, Nigel, as he progressed from infancy through the proto-language into the adult linguistic system.

Let us take as a startingpoint — though it is far from being a startingpoint in relation to the overall development of communicative powers — the observation that, to take part in discourse, a child has to be able to form semantic structures. Discourse as we normally understand it involves the ability to construct, in the mother tongue, sequences that hang together, that in some sense form structures at the semantic or semological level. Typically, there is a time lag such that the child's ability to form semantic structures is always a little bit ahead of his power to create the appropriate grammatical structures that stand as the realization of these semantic structures. Let me illustrate this. There was a time at which Nigel could encode such things as the following (1;7):

> tɹì . . . ʔɔ́ . . . tìkawè: . . . ōgɔ̀ . . . bāba̅

Translated 'word for word', this meant *tree . . . broken . . . take-away . . . all-gone . . . bye-bye*. Semantically speaking, it can fairly be considered to form a single whole. It represents a kind of narrative, in which the child is proceeding from one event to another in a way which makes the whole thing into a coherent piece of discourse. But he is not yet able to encode this in any kind of grammatical structure. Grammatically it is a string of five distinct elements, and it will be some time before Nigel's ability to construct grammatical structures has caught up with this — by which time, of course, he will have become able to create much more complex semantic structures, so that for a long time there is going to be a developmental gap between the two.

As it happened, it was possible to follow fairly closely the steps by which Nigel's semantic structures gradually became grammaticalized, at least at this very early stage. We can I think follow the general tradition in language development studies and take the intonation contour as the manifestation of grammatical structure. A complex utterance produced on a single intonation contour is considered to function as a grammatical unit. Evidence in favour of this interpretation can be seen in Nigel's own discourse, which shows a clear progression from combinations of elements that are semantically well-formed but spoken on two separate intonation contours, to combinations of the same elements, spoken this time on a single contour. For example, Nigel progresses in a short time from:

> là . . . là gɹì

'Light . . . light, green' (with no pause between the last two) — all unlinked grammatically — to, two days later:

> gɹì: . . . gɹì:là

'Green . . . green light'. And I take it that the last of these:

> gɹ̄ì:là

represents a grammatical structure, in which the tone contour
that Nigel always associates with utterances having this general
function — a mid falling tone — is now spread over the whole
combination of two elements, rather than being associated
as it was in the first instance with each of the elements in turn.
At this point (1;7) we now have the following as examples of
semantic structures which are grammatically coded, that is to
say represented as single grammatical structures:

g.ɹiːkà

'Green car';

tʉːbɔ̀kʷ

'Two books';

mɔ́ːmɪ̀ʔ

'More meat'. The following, however, while coded at the
semantic level, are not yet coded at the level of grammatical
structure, so they are intonationally discontinuous:

tʃò̯ya . . . là . . . g.ɹì

'Train, light, green' (the train passed and the light went green)

ⁿdàⁿda . . . pàɪ . . . [blowing] ɸʷ . . . ʈʼò̯ya

'Uncle, pipe, smoke, train' (uncle's pipe makes smoke like a
train).

By the time a child is facing this particular task, of developing simultaneously his ability to construct semantic structures
and his ability to encode these lexicogrammatically, he is
already engaged in acts of meaning of considerable complexity.
He already has behind him some 18 months' experience of
communicating and probably around 12 months' experience
of meaning. I am making a distinction here between communicative acts in general, which the child is engaging in from birth,
and what may be called *acts of meaning*. An act of meaning is
not only directed to another person; it is also symbolic: it is
an act that is characterized by the intent to communicate
symbolically. I think this distinction is an important one,
even though we shall find it difficult on occasions to say
whether a given instance fulfils this criterion or not; there

are intermediate cases between acts that are symbolically mediated and acts that are not. It was at the age of six months that Nigel proclaimed his ability to engage in symbolic communicative acts, or acts of meaning, when he first gave expression to an interest in his surroundings; attention to some form of visual prominence, particularly birds flying or a similar commotion. This he did by means of a high-pitched squeak, which he addressed to us frequently in such contexts for a period of about four weeks, during which time it was his only act that would satisfy the criterion of being an act of meaning; after that it totally disappeared. The effect was almost as if the child had been using this occasion to register the fact that he was now an independent participant in the interactive process of meaning; that he could not only respond, but could actually initiate the process, and bring about responses on the part of his mother or other interlocutor. Be that as it may, he had established the principle that he could mean; having once done so, he decided that it was not yet affording him much scope, and stopped it. This is typical of many developmental steps, where one first has a kind of trailer, a preview of what is to come, then an interlude, and then the full step is taken in earnest.

When Nigel did engage in acts of meaning, systematically, he began at just under nine months with a small set of symbolic gestures, which illustrate in a rather interesting way the transition from non-symbolic to symbolic acts. In a pragmatic context, and specifically in the instrumental function of wanting objects, Nigel developed a gesture whereby if he was offered some object that he did not want, he would touch it very briefly and very lightly with one finger and then take the finger away. There was no pushing – he was not distancing the object in any sense; it was a symbolic gesture addressed to another person and meaning 'I don't want that; take it away'. This sign clearly satisfies the criterion of intent to communicate symbolically; but it has a slightly iconic flavour, as is brought out by its relation to another gesture with which it contrasted. If Nigel did want the object, then he grasped it firmly – and then let go, without trying to pull it towards him. This is clearly non-arbitrary, in relation to the meaning of 'I want'; but again it was addressed to another person, and was clearly distinguished from the simple act of actually grabbing the object and pulling it towards him. So at the age of nine months Nigel developed a little system of acts of meaning expressed through the medium of gesture. But he was a child who preferred the vocal medium and he decided after a few weeks that this rich noise-producing mechanism that he had would provide a more effective means of expression; so he started constructing a typical infant proto-language made of sound, or vocal gesture. This took over from the little gestural system, and all gestures disappeared except for one which remained throughout the protolinguistic period, namely the demand for music, which took the form of 'beating time'. This meant 'Put the record player on' or 'Sing me a song', in other words 'Produce music somehow or other'; this was perhaps a little too abstract to encode in vocal form and needed some iconic representation. Nigel's other acts of meaning were encoded in vocal mode, and over the next six months he built up a proto-language that I have written about in detail elsewhere. This included, at the start, signs such as

nananana

meaning, 'I want that, give me that', and

ə

meaning 'Do that again'. The latter, while still pragmatically oriented (language as action), was regulatory rather than instrumental in function, since it was directed towards the behaviour of a particular person; and it illustrates an early form of proto-texture. If someone was playing with him or entertaining him in some way and then stopped, Nigel would say:

ə

meaning 'Do it again, go on'. This went on as long as they were willing to resume. When they finally stopped, and Nigel realized that his act or meaning was no longer being successful, he replaced it with a loud

mnŋ

meaning 'Do that again, or else!'. This functioned as a kind of intensified form of the same sign.

By the age of ten and a half months Nigel had developed a little language consisting of twelve meanings expressed by vocal gestures which were his own invention. For those interested in nineteenth-century views on the origin of language, probably all of the suggested sources such as 'ding-dong', 'bow-wow' and 'yo-heave-ho' could be illustrated from Nigel's proto-language, as well as the practice of putting to linguistic use sounds that he had heard himself produce naturally. For example, at a very early age he would often go to sleep with his thumb in front of his mouth, producing a sucking noise accompanied by movement of the vocal cords, something like this:

$$\breve{g}^{w}\gamma\iota\breve{g}^{w}\gamma\iota\breve{g}^{w}\gamma\iota$$

— a simple oscillation between the two fundamental postures recognized in prosodic phonology under the names 'y' and 'w'. He had heard himself make this noise and obviously decided it could be put to use in his symbolic system; so some months later we find him saying (i.e., addressing to someone)

$$\breve{g}^{w}\gamma\iota\breve{g}^{w}\gamma\iota\breve{g}^{w}\gamma\iota$$

meaning 'I've had enough — I want to go to sleep', and curling himself up on the floor with his eyes shut.

A little later, at about 13 months, he transferred the same sound to another function; by this time he was beginning to play with language, and he decided that this sound could be transferred to the play function, so he would lie down on the floor, curl himself up, produce the same sound

$$\breve{g}^{w}\gamma\iota\breve{g}^{w}\gamma\iota\breve{g}^{w}\gamma\iota$$

and then gurgle with laughter; 'Let's play that I pretend I'm going to sleep'. It does not really matter where the expressions come from at this stage; the child is developing a proto-semantic system, and the realizations, whether vocal or gestural, can come from anywhere. With some children they may be imitations of words in the adult language; and this is what is liable to confuse the investigator, because he is liable to think that the child has a vocabulary. In fact he is simply using English, or whatever the mother tongue is, as a source for his own sound system; the elements are not words, but syllables.

Now when Nigel comes to make the distinction referred to earlier, between ə̃̀ 'do that again' and the intensified form m̃ǹŋ 'do that again – I insist!', he is beginning to be sensitive to texture. Texture is a particular property that acts of meaning have in the adult world. In addition to its other modes – ideational (the property of being about something) and interpersonal (the property of being between people) – an act of meaning has a third property, which is what literary critics have always referred to as texture, the property of being part of some larger scheme, including other acts of meaning and other features of the social context, the situational and cultural environment. Utterances in the adult language have a textual structure, a textual aspect to their meaning, as well as the other aspects. Nigel's use of a distinct sign to follow-up a 'failed' act of meaning, repeating it with an added component of intensity, represents a very early – perhaps the earliest – awareness of the texture of symbolic interaction.

Henry Widdowson, in his discussion of cohesive procedures, referred to rules of 'usage' on which the cohesive procedures operate, and enumerated a number of these factors that enter into text structure. I propose here to look at the way in which Nigel developed some of these specific abilities; in other words, at how he developed the textual potential in his speech. The process begins surprisingly early. I had assumed, without really thinking about it, that there could be no texture until the child was well launched into the mother tongue – that it was essentially a feature of language, not of proto-language. In fact, it appears that there may be texture in the proto-language also. Perhaps the clearest example came from the 'naming game', which Nigel began at about 15 months, with a sign meaning 'Look at this picture, let's name it together' – it being understood that he knows the name perfectly well and has heard it in this context before. He opens his little board book, points to a coloured picture in it and says:

a͡::dâ [mid rise + mid fall, no upjump]

This is what is going to evolve at the next stage into the meaning 'What's that?', the demand for a name that is unknown; but at this stage it is simply 'You say the name'. So his mother says 'That's a ball'. Nigel then turns over to the next page and he says:

a͡ːdà   [mid rise + (upjump to) high fall]

'And what's *that*?'. Here we have a clear signal that this is a second move; the up-jump and high falling tone show that it is a follow-up to the first exchange. This is already a form of interaction that has texture to it; the relation of this utterance to what preceded it is foregrounded by the use of a special intonation pattern.

Texture is also present, in a special sense, in the kind of reparatory acts that the child engages in, when one of his acts of meaning has failed. We should not be too surprised at the child's early awareness of instances in which the communication process has broken down, when his meaning has not got over. What is interesting is the strategy the child adopts for repairing the breakdown. Nigel developed at an early age (1;6) a strategy that would serve him in such situations for the rest of his life: he learnt to repeat, slowly and clearly, the items that had not been understood. The day after he reached 18 months, he had been out for a walk, and after getting home was rehearsing the things he had seen:

ɢàːꞐɢàːꞐ . . . tìkᵚ . . . lòu . . .bà

'(I saw) ducks, sticks, holes, buses'. The next item in the list was

dòubā

His father, who was responding as he went along, had followed him up to this point; but this defeated him. The expression usually meant 'toast and butter', but it seemed unlikely that Nigel had seen toast and butter on his walk. He tried various guesses, but they were not right, and finally Nigel repeated, very slowly and deliberately:

do̅ubà

— just as if he was talking to someone having difficulty with the language. As it happened, the ruse did not work; his father never did understand. But the pattern was established, and represented a significant step in the development of a texture of verbal interaction.

Let me now illustrate the specific stages through which Nigel built up the elementary text-forming resources of the mother tongue. There are certain semantic patterns that serve to give cohesion to a discourse: reference, substitution, conjunction, reiteration. Nigel began to develop these during the transition from proto-language to mother tongue, roughly the second half of the second year. The first to appear was the demonstrative reference item *that;* and it was used first in a deictic (exophoric) context, referring to the situation, e.g. (1;7):

>   that bròke

meaning 'that thing there'. At the same time, Nigel began regularly using the expressions

>   háve it [or] háve that   a͡vιt,   a͡vdat

accompanied by pointing, meaning 'I want that thing there'. In this period, 19½-21 months, *that* and *it* are exophoric, referring to things in the situation; but there is an interesting example at 1;8 which is in a sense intermediate between exophoric and anaphoric reference, namely

>   that sóng

meaning 'Sing that song you've just been singing'. The progression to fully anaphoric reference is gradual; in 1;8 we have

>   train under túnnel . . . getit fóryou

where the train is only just out of sight, and

>   why that clóck stop . . . ménd it

where the clock is being remembered from some hours earlier, and the whole utterance may be copied from what his father had said at the time. True anaphoric reference is not established until 1;11.

Meanwhile, however, Nigel had another partly anaphoric element at this stage, which was not a reference item but a substitute. This was the word *one*, as it occurs in English in *give me another one* where *one* is a replacement for some noun that the hearer has to supply from the preceding context: he must be able to tell, another what. Nigel uses the substitute *one* first of all in contexts where it is both exophoric and anaphoric at the same time. He is blowing bubbles; a particularly fine bubble appears, and he says:

> big ̀one

(with tonic on *one*, not on *big* as in adult speech). Previous to that the word *bubble* had been used, including by Nigel himself:

> bēbʷ ɹɒuɹɒu

'Bubbles going round and round'. So when he says *big one*, the bubbles have been mentioned before, and they are also there in the context. The same expression was used when he was watching trains go by at the station and a second train came along which was longer than the one before; this time the tonic was on *big*:

> bi̖g one

Again the referent is present in the context; there is still a situational as well as a textual component in the meaning of the substitute *one*.

This particular period, 19½ to 21 months, is critical for Nigel's development of text structure. Here is a little interchange with his mother. Nigel is sitting in his high chair and waiting patiently for his breakfast; he says:

> put bemax down on tа́ble

'Put Bemax down on table'. But the Bemax is already there, on the big table; his mother says 'It is on the table'. Nigel says:

> ni̖la table

'Nigel's table', in other words 'put it on my table'. The sequence is:

> Nigel: Put Bemax down on *table*.
> Mother: It *is* on the table.
> Nigel: *Nigel* table.

Note the intonation pattern, in which the tonic has gone back from its unmarked position on the final lexical item to the lexical item that precedes, thus clearly marking the second occurrence of *table* as related by contrast to the first, exactly

as in an adult utterance. Again as in adult speech, the tone is
not affected; it remains rising, the tone that Nigel is using
at this period for all pragmatic (response-demanding) utterances.
Shortly afterwards, having been warned about the consequences
of banging his trains around, Nigel said:

> that blue train might brèak . . . réd train might break

'That blue train might break; red train might break?' — In
other words, does the rule apply also to the red train? Here
the tonic moves right to the beginning and the whole of the
rest is post-tonic.

These examples show that Nigel has learnt to contrast
different information structures, using a marked form, that
with the tonic in pre-final position, to relate what he is saying
to the preceding discourse. The same pattern appears again
in the following dialogue: Nigel has been out for a walk with
his mother, and when he gets back he looks at her and says
(1;9):

> big nòise

His mother asks 'Who made a big noise?' Nigel answers:

> drìll make big noise

'*Drill* made big noise'. The tonic on *drill* signals that what
follows is 'given' material.

The systematic placing of the tonic also comes into play
when Nigel learns to make lists, for example (1;9):

> one blúe chuffa . . . one rèd chuffa

'One *blue* train, one *red* train'. This involves not only pre-
supposing what has gone before but also anticipating what
is to come; the list must have been planned as a whole.

Shortly after this, Nigel introduces texture of a fourth kind
into his linguistic system, namely conjunction: for example
(1;10):

> thát tree got leaf on but thāt tree got nō lèaf on

This *but* is the first instance of a conjunctive in Nigel's speech;
its function, as in the adult language, is to link the second
clause in a meaningful way to the first. It is the expression of

one of a small number of semantic relations — additive, adversative, causal and temporal — which, taken as a whole, provide an interpretation of each step in the discourse in terms of how it relates to what has gone before.

We have been focussing attention on a stage in language development that is critical because, from a linguistic point of view, it represents a transition. This stage, which corresponds, with Nigel, to the second half of the second year, is the one in which Nigel is moving from the proto-language into the mother tongue; and as part of the process, at the same time as learning to build up the other components of meaning, and the structures to express them, he is also learning to build up this 'textual' or text-forming component.

So far, I have considered texture of two kinds. One was part of the internal organization of the grammatical unit; this was exemplified by Nigel's control of information structure — his ability to assign a focus of information by locating the tonic prominence. The other was the organization of inter-sentence relations of the cohesive type, exemplified by Nigel's use of conjunction, beginning with *but*, and of reference and substitution, beginning with the items *that, it* and *one*; the latter used first exophorically and then, by gradual steps, ana-phorically, in contexts in which there is no deictic element — the object being referred to is not present in the situation and the presupposition relates solely to what has been said before.

We can also see, at this stage, the beginning of the develop-ment of a third and final aspect of texture, namely, generic structure. There are patterns of texture that relate to particular genres. The first generic types to emerge are the broad cate-gories of narrative and dialogue. The narrative mode develops out of one kind of act of meaning, that which I referred to as 'mathetic' (essentially what M.M. Lewis used to call declara-tive): it is an act of meaning that is self-sufficient, calls for no response, and functions as an explicit reality-creating device. The dialogue mode evolves out of pragmatic acts of meaning, which are essentially acts of a kind that demand a response. Both these modes, narrative and dialogue, require that the child should be sensitive to the particular generic structures that are associated with them.

There is an important distinction to be made between

dialogue and communication. As I said at the beginning, I
think we must assume that a child has the ability to communicate in some sense from birth. Dialogue, however, is a special
kind of communication. It is a form of interaction in which
the interactants are adopting, and assigning to one another,
specific roles in the communication process, through which
they exchange information and 'goods and services'. In the
adult language these configurations of roles are expressed by
means of variation in speech function; statement, question,
command, offer and their various derivative categories. These
provide the resources for the ongoing exchange of meaning. So
by dialogue I mean something specific, something that has to
be learned. Nigel is learning dialogue at this time, a process
that we can see exemplified by his ability to verbalize instruc-
tions while carrying them out, to make offers, to respond to
requests, and so forth. And it is interesting to note that, with
Nigel, the learning of dialogue involves strategies that appear,
from the point of view of the adult language, very devious.
They involve him in constructing models of dialogue that do
not correspond to anything in the adult language, and then
have to be reinterpreted and even abandoned when the child
later on takes up the adult mode.

Let us see where Nigel has got to at 1;11, on the eve of his
second birthday, in building up the resources for the internal
organization of texture. Here is a sample of his conversation.
He has a sloping plank that he's using to run trains down;
something has fallen underneath it. Nigel looks and says:

how did that get under thère

He reaches for it and pulls it out; it's a toothbrush. He says:

I wōnder if the train will pulling the tòothbrush

He tries it out. It does; but the toothbrush falls off, and this
time he can't reach it. This situation reminds him of another
toothbrush that he's been allowed to play with, and he says:

have daddy gréen toothbrush

Here *toothbrush* has become post-tonic, showing it is 'given' in
the context, and *green* carries the tonic, the focus of information. The theme is *have*, expressing the speech function 'I

want'; this is a subcategory of the meaning 'action demanded' that is expressed by the rising tone. His father says, 'Yes, you can have Daddy's toothbrush'. Nigel goes on:

> but you càn't have daddy něw toothbrush

Here we have a *but* and two points of information focus, *can't* and *new*; moreover *new* carries the contrastive (fall-rise) tone, which makes explicit its opposition to *green*. This proposition being agreed to, that he can't have Daddy's new toothbrush, Nigel goes on brightly:

> have daddy new toothbrush

Here *have* is again theme, but this time it is also focal; 'I *want* it!'. All that follows the tonic is again 'given', just as in the adult language.

In this exchange we can see the development of Nigel's potential for dialogue: his ability to manipulate the roles defined by verbal interaction. For a final illustration, let us return to the building up of narrative. It is important to stress that narrative, even though it evolves out of the kind of speech act that does not demand a response, is nevertheless a form of interaction, and is typically built up through conversation as an interactive process. Here is an example from age 1;8. Nigel had been taken to the London Zoo, and had gone into the Children's Zoo where he met up with a goat and started to stroke it. In his other hand he was holding a plastic jam jar lid that he had picked up somewhere on the ground and now regarded as his property. The goat worked its way around so that it could nibble at this lid, but the keeper took the lid away, explaining that it wasn't good for the goat to eat. The incident passed off, and about four hours later, back at home, Nigel turns to his father and says:

> try eat lìd

His father says 'What tried to eat the lid?'. And Nigel says again:

> try eat lìd

'What tried to eat the lid?'

> gòat

Then he summarizes these two in one sentence, forming a single grammatical structure:

> goat try eat lĭd

Encouraged to continue the story, he then adds:

> man said nò

This now makes a little narrative, and Nigel runs it through a few times, just to make sure it works:

> goat try eat lĭd . . . man said nò

This is now left aside for another interval, again of about three to four hours, which seems fairly typical of the time taken at this stage for complex experiences to be processed into a verbal form. It is now bath-time, a good time for story-telling; Nigel starts off the same story with his mother and says:

> goat try eat lĭd . . . man said nò

His mother said 'Why did the man say no?'. And he said:

> goat shòuldn't eat lid . . . [shaking head] gòodfor it

At this time Nigel had no negative in a narrative context. He had a pragmatic negative, in the sense of 'I don't want . . .', 'don't . . .!', but no mathetic negative; he could say *shouldn't*, as this was pragmatic in the system, even though being used here in a reported frame, but for 'not' in 'not good for it' he could only shake his head.

At this point, Nigel felt he had the complete story. So in the course of further conversation he goes back to the beginning and produces the whole account in a single utterance:

> goat try eat lĭd . . . man said nò . . . goat shòuldn't eat lid . . . [shaking head] gòodfor it

This story is repeated, verbatim, day after day over the next few months.

I have attempted here to sketch in the genesis of the text-forming component in the semantic system as it appears from the study of the development of speech in one particular child. We have considered each of the three main aspects of textual meaning: (1) the internal texture of the clause, in terms of information and thematic structure, corresponding to the 'functional sentence perspective' of Prague School linguistics; (2) the external 'cohesive' relations of reference, substitution and conjunction; and (3) the generic properties of narrative and dialogue. Only a brief illustration could be given here of the first steps taken by the child in these directions. But the account may serve to indicate how the ability to construct text proceeds alongside the development of ideational and interpersonal meanings, and so contributes to the understanding of the fundamental relation between the code and the text — between language as system and language in use.

Note
See Bibliography under: Daneš (1974); France (1975); Halliday (1975); and Halliday and Hasan (1976)

DEIXIS AND ANAPHORA

The topic that I have chosen to talk about — the relationship between deixis and anaphora — turns out to be even more appropriate than I had hoped.[1] Dr Bullowa, Dr Widdowson and Professor Halliday have all touched upon either deixis or anaphora, or both, in their contributions to the symposium; and they have all made points to which I can refer in the development of the thesis that I am presenting.

I will argue that deixis is both ontogenetically and logically prior to anaphora. By this I mean that the deictic use of pronouns and other such expressions precedes their anaphoric use in the earliest stages of language-acquisition and, furthermore, that anaphora, as a grammatical and semantic process, is inexplicable except in terms of its having originated in deixis. That deixis precedes, and is in some sense more basic than anaphora, is something that the previous speakers would probably concede immediately. But it is not at all uncommon for linguists to describe the meaning of pronouns, as far as possible, in terms of anaphora and to treat that part of the use of pronouns which is irreducibly deictic as a theoretical embarrassment that is best forgotten. It is certainly the case that generative grammarians have been inclined, until recently at least, to underestimate the role played by deixis in the interpretation of utterances; and the very term 'pronominalisation', which figures so prominently in works on generative grammar, is loaded in favour of the view that pronouns are, first and foremost, substitutes for nouns (or nominals).

The primacy of deixis is a principle that can be related very directly to what Dr Bullowa and Professor Halliday had to say about the primacy of gesture, attention and interaction in the acquisition of language. The term 'deixis' is revealing in this connection: it means no more than "pointing" in its original Greek sense; and, as used nowadays by linguists, it means "identification by pointing". Drawing upon work by Bateson and Gruber, Dr Bullowa suggested in her paper that there are two kinds of performatives that can be distinguished among the child's earliest two-word utterances, designations* and requests, and that non-performative (i.e., constative) utterances come later. She went on to demonstrate that pointing is developmentally indistinguishable from reaching and that, in so far as the child designates what he is requesting by looking at it, reaching and looking tend to coincide, as do designation and requesting; and that they too are originally indistinguishable.[2] Professor Halliday, for his part, emphasised, as others have done, that the child's earliest semiotic acts are gestural, rather than vocal, and that the earliest exophoric (i.e., deictic) expressions tend to be accompanied with a gesture indicative of attention. I need not remind you that there is some similarity between this way of analysing the proto-semantic system of the child and the famous tripartite analysis of the functions of language by Bühler (1934), which was taken over by Roman Jakobson and other linguists of the Prague School. It was Bühler, too, you will recall, who popularised, if he did not actually coin, the term 'deixis' in the sense in which it is employed these days (not to mention the terms 'cataphora' and 'exophora'): and my views on deixis and anaphora have been strongly influenced by his. They have also been influenced by the now classic articles by Benveniste (1956) and Hjelmslev (1937) on the nature of pronouns; by the work of Antinucci (1974) and Bates (1976); and, even more directly, by the ideas of my colleagues who worked on the SSRC-sponsored language-acquisition project in Edinburgh (cf. Huxley 1970, Atkinson and Griffiths 1973, Lyons, et al 1975).

The general point that I draw from the papers by Dr Bullowa and Professor Halliday is that the child's earliest semiotic behaviour is very largely gestural (in the broadest sense of 'gestural') and is, in any case, so closely integrated with other kinds of attentive, conative, manipulative and desiderative behaviour as to be indistinguishable from it. But

---

*Editor's Note: Dr Bullowa has subsequently used the term 'indication' in the edited version of her paper.

I also draw the more specific point that there are very many
semiotic acts, whether gestural or vocal, of which it is impossible
to say that their function is primarily that of designating,
of requesting or of reporting. It is only when you get a more
or less fully-developed adult language-system that these three
kinds of speech-acts can be clearly and confidently distinguished.
Now, Dr Bullowa talked of proto-conversations and Professor
Halliday of proto-sentences (and proto-semantics). Not wishing
to be outdone by these two protagonists, I will now introduce
the term 'proto-reference'. Elsewhere, I have used the term
'quasi-reference' (cf. Lyons 1975); but 'proto-reference' is
perhaps better. Proto-reference is to be identified with what
we have just been calling 'designation'.

The main point that I want to make — and I have made it
before (Lyons 1975) — is that proto-reference, which rests
crucially upon the psychological notion of attention, might
equally well be called 'proto-predication'. When linguists and
logicians analyse the propositional content of utterances, and
more particularly of constative utterances, within the framework of formal semantics, they commonly begin by distinguishing two components: the referential component, which
identifies the entity (or entities) about which something is
is being said, and the predicative component, which says whatever it is that is said about the referent (or referents). The
underlying notion of the bipartite structure of propositions
goes back a long way, of course; and it has given rise to the
familiar and related distinctions of subject *vs* predicate and
topic *vs* comment (or theme *vs* rheme). I do not wish to go
into this question. What I want to do here is to stress that, as
far as the early utterances of children are concerned, it is very
often impossible to distinguish reference from predication: one
cannot say that the child is referring to something in the situation and leaving implicit what he wants to say about it or,
alternatively, that he is leaving implicit his reference to some
entity in the situation and making explicit what he wants to
say about it. It is only later that reference and predication can
be distinguished; and they may be thought of as developing
ontogenetically from something, proto-reference or proto-
predication, that is originally not clearly the one or the other.
The constative function of language, important though it is,

must not be assumed, by virtue of the philosopher's very natural concern with truth and factuality, to be either basic or ubiquitous, as it all too often is assumed to be.

There are two more preliminary points that I must make — both of them terminological — before I move on to my main theme. The first has to do with the notion of anaphoric reference. It is traditional to say that a pronoun refers to its antecedent. There is, however, an alternative formulation, based on a quite different sense of the term 'refer', according to which we can say that an anaphoric pronoun is co-referential with its antecedent: that is, that an anaphoric pronoun refers to what its antecedent refers to. It is this second formulation of the notion of anaphoric reference that we will adopt: it has the advantage of bringing anaphoric reference within the scope of the current philosophical concept of reference: and, what is far more important for our present purpose, it enables us to relate anaphora and deixis in terms of a single univocal notion of pronominal reference.

The second terminological point has to do with the implications of the term 'pronoun'. According to the traditional conception of the syntactic and semantic function of pronouns, the pronoun is essentially a noun-substitute; and the term 'pronoun' itself reflects this conception of their function. However, to say that pronouns deputise, as it were, for nouns — that the pronomen deputised for the nomen rather as the proconsuls deputised abroad for the consuls — and that this is their primary, or basic, syntactic and semantic function, is misleading in two respects. First of all, it implies that the anaphoric function of pronouns is more basic than their deictic function: we need say no more about this. Second, it fails to draw the distinction between nouns and nominals — between *N*'s and *NP*'s, to use the now more or less well-established symbols of Chomskyan generative grammar. This distinction, as it happens, is less obvious (as is the distinction between names and nouns) in Latin than it is in many other languages, including English, where countable nouns in the singular do not normally occur in referring expressions unless they are accompanied by a determiner or quantifier. But from a theoretical point of view the distinction is crucial. Nominals (e.g., *John* or *that boy*), unlike nouns (e.g., *boy*), have as their most characteristic function that of referring to, or otherwise identifying (e.g., by summoning or listing), particular entities or groups of entities: nouns, on the other hand, are characteristically predicative in function; and the most typical nouns are sortal, rather than characterising, predicates (in the logician's sense of 'predicate': cf. Strawson 1975). The term 'pronoun', unhyphenated, is now so well entrenched in the everyday vocabulary that nothing but confusion would result from any attempt to dislodge it or narrow its application. What we can do, however, is to introduce, as many linguists have done, a set of hyphenated technical terms: 'pro-noun', 'pro-nominal', 'pro-verb', 'pro-verbal', 'pro-adjective', etc.

All of these terms, and others, have been employed by scholars working in the Bloomfieldian tradition (cf. Crymes 1968); and they have the advantage that they make transparent the defining syntactic relation that holds between nouns and pro-nouns (cf. *book* and *one* in *the red book and the blue one*); between nominals and pro-nominals (cf. *John* and *he* in *When John came in, he was grinning all over his face*, on the assumption that *he* and *his*, refer to what *John* refers to); between adjectives and pro-adjectives (cf. *beautiful* and *so* in *Mary is beautiful and so is Penelope*); etc. Armed with these distinctions, we may note that of the text-forming devices mentioned by Professor Halliday, in his paper, the pro-nominals (*that, it* etc.) were characteristically exophoric, or deictic, whereas the pro-noun, *one*, was anaphoric. There is reason to believe that the notion of anaphora applies rather differently to pro-nouns than it does to pro-nominals; and that pro-adjectives and pro-verbs (e.g., *do* in some uses) are like pro-nouns, whereas pro-locatives (*here* and *there*) and pro-temporals (*now* and *then*), are like pro-nominals. I will restrict my attention, in what follows, to pro-nominals: that is, to what are traditionally described as demonstrative and personal pronouns. But I would also emphasise that there is a very close semantic connection between pro-nominals and pro-locatives, on the one hand, and between pro-locatives and pro-temporals, on the other.

As nominals and pro-nominals are, characteristically, entity-referring expressions, so locatives and pro-locatives are, characteristically, place-referring expressions. Entities are not places and places are not entities. However, as I have emphasised elsewhere (cf. Lyons 1975), it is very difficult to draw a sharp distinction between entity-referring and place-referring expressions in the earliest utterances of children; and this fact is of considerable importance for the proper understanding of deixis, of the transition from deixis to anaphora, and also of the emergent distinction of reference and predication. I cannot go into all this here (cf. Lyons 1977). Let me simply say that gestures obviously do not make it clear whether the attention of the addressee is being directed to a region of the environment in which something is happening or to some entity that is located in the environment: and this is one of the reasons why purely ostensive definition necessarily fails of its purpose, unless it is supplemented in some other way. English is a language in which there is a fairly clear distinction, in most instances, between entity-referring and place-referring expressions, But this distinction depends in turn upon the clear distinction that there is in English between the demonstrative pronouns (i.e., pro-nominals) *this* and *that*, on the one hand, and the demonstrative adverbs (i.e., pro-locatives) *here* and *there*, on the other. The proto-referential *Bird*! ("Look! A bird!") has a certain ambivalence as between one interpretation, expressed in the adult language by means of *That's a bird*, and another, expressed by means of *There's a bird*. Until the distinction between entity-referring and place-referring deictics has become established, it cannot really be said to mean the one thing rather than the other. If I mention these questions here, it is merely to indicate that, in the necessarily brief account of the relationship between deixis and anaphora that I am giving in my contribution to the symposium, there is a good deal of more or less metaphysical underpinning that I am taking for granted.

As we have just seen, we can refer, in principle, either to entities or to places by means of deictic expressions. What counts as an entity I take to be at least partly determined independently of the lexical and grammatical structure of the languages that we happen to speak. In particular, I assume that there are what I will refer to as first-order entities (persons, animals and discrete physical objects); that, in so far as the child refers to entities, rather than places, in the earliest stages of language-acquisition, it is to such first-order entities that he refers; that all languages will provide the means for referring to first-order entities; and that reference to first-order entities is a more basic kind of reference than is reference to various kinds of higher-order entities. All these assumptions are, as far as I know, reasonable in the light of what we know of language-acquisition and of the structure of various languages. Apart from first-order entities, there are also second-order and third-order entities to be reckoned with, though it may well be the case that not all languages provide the means for reference to them as entities. By second-order entities I mean events, situations and states-of-affairs occurring or existing in the physical world; and by third-order entities, in so far as we are concerned with them here, I mean such intensional objects as propositions, individual concepts and the like. The importance of third-order entities, for our present purposes, is that, regardless of whether we have the means of referring to them as entities or not, they are the stuff of which the universe-of-discourse is made; and anaphora, as we shall see, depends crucially upon the universe-of-discourse. It may be observed in passing that the traditional distinction of concrete and abstract nouns in terms of their occurrence in expressions referring to concrete and abstract entities tends to obscure the distinction between second-order and third-order entities. There is a sense in which events are more abstract than persons; but there is nothing non-physical about events, as there is about propositions. It is the tripartite ontological distinction that we have just drawn, rather than the traditional bipartite distinction of concrete and abstract, that is important for semantic analysis.

Distinctions of proximity are lexicalised or grammaticalised in the pro-nominal (and pro-locative) system of many languages; and they are commonly combined with other distinctions, based, as far as reference to first-order entities is concerned, on status, sex, shape, size etc. It is the function of pro-nominals, when they are used deictically with reference to first-order and second-order entities, to draw the attention of the addressee to referents that are actually present in the situation, identifying these referents for the addressee in terms of their proximity or remoteness relative to the spatio-temporal zero-point of the deictic space. Since third-order entities have no spatio-temporal location, they cannot be referred to deictically in the way that first-order and second-order entities can. It is important to realise, however, that, although third-order entities are not present either in the situation of utterance or in the text, they are, or may be, present in the universe-of-discourse. Furthermore, they are ordered hierarchically in the universe-of-discourse in terms of salience. By this I mean that, at any one time and for any one person, certain entities are more probable candidates for reference than others are; and the intensional objects in correspondence with these entities in the universe-of-discourse are correspondingly more salient. The intensional correlates of first-order entities in the universe-of-discourse I take to be individual concepts (cf. Carnap 1956: 41): the intensional correlates of second-order entities I take to be propositions. Our problem is to account for the transition from deixis to anaphora, given that the basic deictic distinction, in many languages at least, is one of proximity *vs* remoteness. In doing so, we will draw upon the notion of salience in the universe-of-discourse; and we will relate this to the notion of previous mention, which is more commonly invoked in standard treatments of anaphora.

The link between the deictic and the anaphoric use of pro-nominals can be seen in what I will call textual deixis.[3] Demonstrative pronouns and other deictic expressions may be employed to refer to linguistic entities of various kinds in the co-text of an utterance. Consider the following text, for example:

(*A* says) *That's a ptarmigan, isn't it?*
(*B* says) *A what? Spell it for me.*

The referent of *it* in *B*'s utterance is obviously not the same as the referent of *it* (and of *that*) in *A*'s utterance. The referent of *it* in *B*'s utterance is the form *ptarmigan*: only forms may be spelled (or pronounced). Now the function of *it* in *B*'s utterance is not anaphoric, although at first sight it might appear to be: it is not co-referential with, but actually refers to, an antecedent form. (For simplicity of exposition, I am disregarding at this point the distinction between forms and expressions, which a more careful treatment of reference would need to take account of: cf. Lyons 1977.) Textual deixis is frequently confused with anaphora, by virtue of the traditional formulation of the notion of pronominal reference, according to which the pronoun is said to refer to its antecedent, and the failure to distinguish clearly between linguistic and non-linguistic entities.

At one remove from pure textual deixis, though not as clearly distinct from it as anaphora, is the relationship that holds between a referring expression and such third-order entities as propositions. This may be exemplified by means of the following text:

(*A* says) *Harold Wilson has just resigned.*

(*B* says) *Who told you that?*

It is clear that *that* in *B*'s utterance does not refer to the sentence uttered by *A*, but rather to the proposition expressed by *A* in the utterance of the sentence. The proposition does not occur in the text, in any literal sense of 'occur'; it cannot therefore be referred to deictically. At the same time, by virtue of the peculiarly intimate and almost symbiotic relation that holds between sentences and propositions, one can refer to propositions by referring, apparently, to the sentences used in expressing them. The function of *that* in *B*'s utterance would seem to fall somewhere between anaphora and deixis; and it partakes of the characteristics of both: its function, I will say, is that of impure textual deixis. It is not always easy to draw the distinction between pure and impure textual deixis in particular instances; and textual deixis, of which there are many other kinds that I have not exemplified, provides us, I would suggest, with the sort of transitional referential mechanism that we are looking for to take us from ordinary deixis to anaphora.

The demonstratives *this* and *that* in English may be used deictically, not only to refer to first-order entities in the situational context and to linguistic entities of various kinds (whose ontological status we need not here go into) in the text or co-text, but also to refer to events (i.e., second-order entities) that have already occurred, are occurring or are going to occur in the future. The conditions that govern the selection of *this* and *that* with reference to events immediately preceding and immediately following the utterance, or the part of the utterance in which *this* and *that* occur, are quite complex. They include a variety of subjective factors (such as the speaker's dissociation of himself from the event that he is referring to), which are intuitively relatable to the deictic notion of proximity *vs* remoteness, but are difficult to specify precisely. What does seem clear, however, is that the use of the demonstratives in both temporal and textual deixis, and also in anaphora, is connected with their use in spatial deixis. This is more obviously so in many languages other than English. For example, in Latin the pronoun (or adjective) *ille* ("that") is used anaphorically to refer to the referent of the more remote of two potential antecedents and *hic* ("this") is used to refer to the referent of the nearer of two potential antecedents: and they can be translated (into somewhat stilted English) as "the former" and "the latter", respectively. The same is true of the German *jener: dieser* (though *jener* is perhaps also rather stilted in present-day German, the Spanish *ese* (or *aquel*): *este*, the French *celui-là: celui-çi*, the Turkish *o: bu*, and so on. It is the notion of relative proximity in time to the zero-point of utterance that connects anaphora and textual deixis with deictic temporal-reference. Proximity in space is re-interpreted as proximity in time: and proximity in the text or co-text is based upon proximity in time.

So much is clear enough, in a general sort of way. The basically deictic component in an anaphoric expression directs the attention of the addressee to a certain region of the text or co-text and tells him, as it were, that he will find the referent there. But it is not of course the referent itself that he will find in the text or co-text. What he will find is some appropriate antecedent, which will identify the referent for him, typically by naming or describing it.

It is when we come to spell out the details of what is involved in anaphora that it is revealed as something that is both more complex and theoretically more interesting than it appears to be at first sight. For anaphora, as I mentioned earlier, depends for its operation, not only upon the existence of text and co-text, but also upon the existence of an intersubjective

universe-of-discourse. Many French structuralists, like Kristeva
(1969) and Barthes (1970), have insisted that what is commonly
referred to as intersubjectivity should be more properly
described as intertextuality, on the grounds that the shared
knowledge that is applied to the interpretation of text is
itself the product of other texts (cf. Ducrot and Todorov
1972; Culler 1975: 139). Up to a point this is true; and
especially in so far as the intersubjective knowledge that is
required for the interpretation of literary texts is concerned.
But not all the intersubjective knowledge that is exploited
in the construction and interpretation of texts derives from
what has been previously mentioned in other texts. Furthermore, it seems clear from what we know of the way that our
beliefs and assumptions are stored in long-term memory that
they are not stored as text. They may of course be stored, as
propositions, in some kind of quasi-linguistic form. But the
sets and subsets of propositions that comprise our beliefs
and knowledge will not have the property of cohesion (as
distinct from what Dr Widdowson calls coherence). Since
a very considerable part of the intersubjective universe-of-
discourse is stored, presumably, in the long-term memory of
the participants (speaker and addressee, or writer and reader),
it follows that the universe-of-discourse is not stored as a text.
At the same time, it must be recognised that much of the
information that is contained in the universe-of-discourse is
derived from texts. What is more important for our present
purposes, it must also be acknowledged that, over the short
term at least, the universe-of-discourse has some kind of
temporal structure, which is created by the text and con-
tinuously modified by the text. Anaphora depends upon
this fact.

The entities in the universe-of-discourse, it will be recalled,
are third-order entities: they are the intensional correlates of
the referents of linguistic expressions. More specifically,
individual concepts are the intensional correlates of first-order
entities and propositions are the intensional correlates of
second-order entities. I am aware, of course, that the ontological
status of propositions, and still more of individual concepts,
is highly controversial. But we need not be concerned here
with this question: we can treat individual concepts and

propositions as theoretical constructs whose psychological correlates, if they have any, are for our present purposes irrelevant. One way of thinking of individual concepts is as addresses in some computer-file that is serving as a model of the universe-of-discourse. For simplicity of exposition, if for no other reason, we will adopt this point of view. Furthermore, we will assume: i) that the accessibility of the addresses reflects the degree of salience that each address (i.e. each individual concept) currently has in the universe-of-discourse; and ii) that there is stored at each address a set of propositions of which the individual concept whose address it is is a constituent. For example, given that there is, in the intersubjective universe-of-discourse, an individual concept, which we may symbolise (with double quotation-marks) as "Napoleon", there will be stored at the appropriate address such propositions as "Napoleon was a Corsican", "Napoleon invaded Russia", "Napoleon was victorious at Austerlitz", "Napoleon was defeated at Waterloo", and so on. In this case, as in the case of very many of the first-order entities, and especially persons, that we have occasion to identify frequently, there is a well-known and widely-used proper name, *Napoleon*, which, though it is not a uniquely-referring expression (and very few names are), will, by virtue of the salience of "Napoleon", generally be taken to refer to Napoleon Bonaparte, unless the salience of the individual concept correlated with some other first-order entity whose name is *Napoleon* has been boosted by reference to him in the text or co-text.

Let us now look at the question of anaphoric reference from this point of view; and let us, for the purpose of illustration, make the counterfactual assumption that the English demonstratives *this* and *that*, when used anaphorically, whether as pronouns or adjectives (cf. Lyons 1975), do no more than encode the distinction of temporal proximity in relation to the moment of utterance. Thus, *this animal*, used as an anaphoric expression, would (under our counterfactual assumption) direct the attention of the addressee to the most accessible individual concept in the universe-of-discourse satisfying the propositional function "x be an animal"; *that animal* would refer to an entity whose intensional correlate is less accessible; and *the animal* would refer to some entity whose intensional correlate satisfies the function "x be an animal", but it would give the addressee no information about the location (i.e., accessibility) of the individual concept correlated with the referent. No such information would be required, of course, if the referent of *the animal* were the only animal that had been previously mentioned or, alternatively, if there were a generally accepted convention that, in default of any information about the location of the appropriate individual concept in the universe-of-discourse, it was to be taken to be the most recently mentioned entity whose correlated individual concept satisfies the descriptive content of the anaphoric expression.

Things are not quite as simple as this illustration might suggest. The anaphoric use of *this* and *that* in English involves other considerations besides the relative proximity of an appropriate antecedent expression to the moment of utterance; and the considerations that determine the anaphoric use of the definite article are also rather more complex than our counter-factual assumptions have made them. The point that is being illustrated, however, is not affected by these deliberate over-simplifications: it is that, independently of whether particular languages make anaphoric use of demonstratives or not, anaphora rests upon the notion of accessibility in the universe-of-discourse; and accessibility, which reflects salience, is in part determined by recency of mention. In so far as recency of mention is itself, as we have seen, a deictically-based notion and is encoded, in one way or another, in the anaphoric pronouns used in particular languages, anaphora rests ultimately upon deixis. *Quod erat demonstrandum*!

However, it requires but little reflection to see that potential referents cannot be indexed solely, or even primarily, in terms of recency of mention or relative order of previous mention. Quite apart from any other factors that might be operative, the limitations of human memory are such that, without having immediate access to a transcript of all that has been said previously (or, alternatively, to some continuously-updated computer-file), we could not operate with a system of ana-phoric reference which was dependent upon our knowledge of the order of mention of all the entities referred to previously in the text and co-text. The temporal structure that is imposed upon the universe-of-discourse by the succession of referring expressions in texts (which we have assumed to be transformed directly into accessibility) is, therefore, of very limited duration; and the anaphoric use of the basically deictic distinction of proximity to the zero-point of the context of utterance is determined by this fact.

As we have seen, salience in the universe-of-discourse is not determined solely by recency of mention of the correlated non-intensional entity. Indeed, there need not have been any previous mention in any determinate part of the text or co-text. This is obviously so as far as reference by means of proper names, titles or definite descriptions which uniquely identify well-known persons like Napoleon is concerned. But even pronouns can be used to refer to previously-unmentioned entities that are not present in the situation of utterance, provided that the individual concept associated with the entity in question is sufficiently salient in the universe-of-discourse. For example, I might offer my condolences to a friend, whose wife has just been killed in a car crash, by saying: *I was terribly upset to hear the news: I only saw her last week*. On the assumption that my friend and I had not previously discussed the accident and that I had heard the news from someone else, there has been no previous mention of her in the co-text (i.e., in some text or set of texts to which both my friend and I have had access). And yet, in these circumstances, there is absolutely no need for me to specify what news I am referring to or who the referent of *her* is. Many scholars, including Bühler (1934), would say that the reference of pronouns in examples like this is deictic, not anaphoric, on the grounds that there is no antecedent and that, although it does not point to anything in the external situational context, it does point to something in the intersubjective experience or common memory of speaker and addressee (cf. Crymes 1968: 62-3). It is obvious, however, that the notion of intersubjective experience or common memory — formalisable as part of the universe-of-discourse — is the more general notion, without which anaphoric reference, as it is traditionally conceived, cannot be explained. In the last resort, there seems to be no reason to deny that the reference of *her* in the example that has just been given is anaphoric.

It is not possible, on the present occasion, to develop the

thesis that anaphora depends ultimately upon deixis in any
greater detail than this. Both deixis and anaphora are far more
complex, of course, than the somewhat schematic account of
them that I have given here. What has been said will be sufficient, it is hoped, to give some indication of the way in which
a satisfying explanation of the ontogenesis of anaphora might
be constructed. As we have seen, anaphora presupposes that
the intensional correlate of the referent should already have
its place in the universe-of-discourse. Deixis does not: indeed
deixis is one of the principal means open to us of putting the
intensional correlates of entities into the universe-of-discourse
(cf. Isard 1975b); and this fact alone would make deixis
logically, if not ontogenetically, prior to anaphora.

What has been no more than adumbrated in this paper,
however, is the ontogenetic relationship between deixis and
anaphora. I have suggested that textual deixis, pure and
impure, may serve as the link between the two. But I can
hardly claim to have demonstrated that this is so; and I do
not yet know whether the data that has now been collected
by the various research teams working on child-language
acquisition would support the hypothesis that textual deixis
is the precursor of anaphora, as I am suggesting that it is. It
may be pointed out, however, that this hypothesis would
be compatible (to put it no more strongly than this) with
the more general hypothesis, of a broadly Piagetian character,
which informs a good deal of the more recent psycholinguistic
research: the hypothesis that cognitive structures result from
the internalisation of sensori-motor action-schemata (cf.
Bruner 1974/5). Much of my own understanding of the
implications of this hypothesis comes from reading the work
of Elizabeth Bates and her collaborators (cf. Bates 1976);
and it seems to me that she has made a good case for the
view that what she calls metapragmatics (including talking
about talking and referring back to what one has said) plays
a crucial role in the child's reconstruction of his sensori-motor
knowledge of the world at the level of internal, symbolic
representation. However that may be, it seems to me that any
account of the ontogenesis of anaphoric reference has got
to address itself to the problem of explaining how intensional
objects in the universe-of-discourse come to be indexed, at

least partly and over the short term, in terms of the relative order of the associated linguistic expressions occurring in the text (and co-text). As far as I know, the stages of the process whereby this comes about have yet to be identified.

Notes

1. Part of this paper is taken, with certain changes and amplifications, from volume 2 of my book on semantics (Lyons 1977).
2. Bates (1976) argues that the data which she worked with at the Instituto di Psicologia, CNR, Rome, do not support the hypothesis that reaching and pointing have the same ontogenetic source (cf. also Werner and Kaplan 1963). It suffices for the thesis that I am maintaining that the use of some kind of attention-drawing devices (pointing, line-of-sight etc.) should develop early enough to serve as the basis for the subsequent emergence of linguistic deixis. As far as I know, this is not disputed (cf. Bruner 1974/75).
3. In an interesting recent paper R. Lakoff (1974) equates what she calls 'discourse deixis' with anaphora; her discussion of the question is less precise than it might have been, by virtue of her equivocal use of the term 'reference' and her failure to distinguish between linguistic and non-linguistic entities. Her paper also relates what she describes as 'emotional deixis' (for which I prefer the term 'empathetic deixis': cf. Lyons 1977) to spatial deixis and anaphora.

REFLECTIONS ON THE SYMPOSIUM

One is struck with the pioneering nature of the work from Dr Bullowa's laboratory, both in terms of its methodology and its central assumptions. We now see work flourishing in the area of pre-speech, or proto-language (cf. Waterson and Show 1977), within the ethological paradigm that is evolving to a large degree from Bullowa's and Bateson's work. More important, two assumptions I see guiding that early work have proved critical in determining current developments in discourse acquisition studies. I think both are well motivated.

In its assumption that the newborn is a social, communicative being, one may now see the beginnings of a broad revaluation of the Piagetian assumption (Piaget 1926, Vygotsky 1962) of initial communicative egocentricity. More recently, that revaluation has been associated with some startling discoveries about the conversationally finely-adjusted nature of even very young children's talk. Let me briefly review a few of those that seem to bear on the question of communicative egocentricity.

Keenan (1974) suggests in a study of a pair of twin boys aged 2;9 that very young children can and will work to achieve sustained, coherent dialogue by means of attending to the propositional content of a partner's preceding utterance, to its illocutionary force (Searle 1969), to its information structure in terms of given and new information, and even, in the case of sound play, to its phonological form. Hence:

  A. wake up / wake up
  B. [he:kʌt] (laughing)
  A. [he:kʌt]
  B. [be:kʌp]
  A. [bre:kʌt] [bre:kʌp]
  B. wake up / [wi:kʌp] (laughing) [wi:kʌp]

Garvey and Hogan (1973) discovered a high level of mutual responsiveness with eighteen 3½ to 5-year-old dyads, both in terms of speech and behaviour. Despite many instances of egocentric speech and collective monologuing, they found that the vast majority of utterances in their samples were 'in focus' socially, and that many older dyads displayed surprisingly sophisticated 'rhetorical gambits' in order to sustain conversation. All the children's conversations were shown to employ a conventionally-structured series of moves.

More recently, Keenan (1975) has proposed that so-called imitations in child speech, usually regarded as asocial in function at best, can often be taken as pragmatically entirely appropriate speech acts when viewed in their conversational contexts.

Until fairly recently, it had been assumed that even school-aged children could be expected, for cognitive-developmental reasons, to experience difficulty adjusting propositional content of utterances to the information needs of a hearer (Flavell, et al. 1968). In short, they were taken to have had difficulty with *role-taking*, a set of skills that entails a fairly high degree of cognitive decentration. Flavell and associates claimed that role-taking skills (which I think we may assume will underpin socially-adjusted language use) are, even by school age, 'severely limited, though probably not nil'. These claims too are undergoing radical reassessment. Masangky and associates (1974) show that two- and three-year-olds can indeed demonstrate at least minimal appreciation of the existence of visual perspectives other than their own. Some recent work (Reeder 1975a, b) demonstrates that children by age 3;0 can use contextually-inferred assumptions about participant knowledge, intent, and attitudes concerning possible states of affairs, in order to interpret utterances as instances of particular speech acts.

Shatz and Gelman (1973) demonstrate strikingly how four-year-old speakers will adjust the lexical and syntactic complexity of their speech differentially when addressing two-year-old and adult hearers respectively. And a recent reanalysis of their data (Gelman and Shatz 1977) along semantic lines shows, among other things, that these four-year-olds used cognitive verbs (*think, know, feel*, etc.) much less frequently in their 'mental state' senses and more often in their 'hedge' sense when addressing the two-year-olds. Their analysis not only posits intuitive semantic understanding of the various uses of cognitive verbs, but suggests that this very understanding is sufficiently reflexive for its presence or absence to be attributed by the child to an audience.

The weight of the evidence seems to be, then, in favour of attributing even to very young children quite subtle intuitions concerning the linguistic and cognitive capacity and state of a conversational co-participant. In short, claims of initial communicative egocentricity have been seriously, and I think successfully challenged by work proceeding from assumptions of initial sociocentricity of the very sort espoused by Dr Bullowa in her discussion.

The second guiding assumption I see underlying the work that Dr Bullowa reports is that an adequate understanding of the development of conversational skills will not be achieved without reference to a more general theory of the ontogenesis of intentional action.

This assumption is perhaps best exemplified in Gruber's work, and I should like to focus attention on some of the issues raised by his analysis of Dr Bullowa's material. I suspect that some of Gruber's claims warrant clarification, and in so doing I shall refer to the fuller of the two published reports to which Dr Bullowa alluded (Gruber 1975).

First, it is important to clarify the sense in which Gruber employed Austin's 'performative-constative' distinction. Where the distinction of Austin's treatment (1962) was initially, at least, a distinction at the level of intentional action, as between *performing an act verbally* (betting, vowing, pronouncing judgment, etc.) and *saying something* about a state of affairs in the world, Gruber sees a performative element to be a necessary and universal element in linguistic deep structure for *any* utterance (cf. Ross 1970), and claims that such an element is ontogenetically prior to other classes of linguistic elements. Where Gruber makes the performative-constative distinction is at the level of superficial linguistic structure, in terms of the way in which performative and non-performative elements of underlying semantic structure become realised lexically and grammatically. For Gruber, every potential utterance will be, at a deeper level of analysis, performative, but only some will realise in superficial linguistic structure one or more categories (speaker, hearer, performative verb, direct object) from the obligatory underlying performative clause or hypersentence.

Now Gruber found evidence for the hypothesis that at the earliest period of spontaneous multi-word utterances, the only forms realised in surface structure will be obligatory elements from the underlying performative hypersentences, two of which seemed to exhaust the performative repertoire, 'I indicate to you X' and 'I demand of you Y'. Thus, for the first nine weeks of Dory's multi-word utterances, he found things like *see allgone* realising the putative underlying structure 'I indicate to you S', where the embedded S was expanded, by means of rich contextual interpretation, along the lines of 'the shoe is allgone'. Only later can this underlying structure's embedded S be more finely analysed lexically by the child, to emerge as *shoe allgone*. But this later version of the underlying semantic structure above is no less an act with words; all it lacks is the hitherto-obligatory realisation of an element from the performative clause 'I indicate to you S'.

Lest Gruber's formal distinction as reported by Dr Bullowa be taken as a vacuous one, let me underline the relevance of Gruber's analysis to an understanding of the development of conversational competence. Assuming, with Gruber, the applicability of the performative analysis to development questions, the tenth week of Dory's multi-word utterances appears to mark a critical developmental milestone. It is no longer necessary for the child to mark explicitly the illocutionary intent behind the utterance, either with the performative verb itself, or with reference to speaker or hearer. Rather, the illocutionary force of an utterance can now be conveyed indirectly. Notice that there is no principled way of deciding on purely linguistic grounds whether *shoe allgone* is to be heard as an indication, a demand, or whatever. From this point onward, interpretation of utterance intention in such cases must employ contextually-derived inferences in addition to linguistic evidence, and both must be compared in some way against sets of felicity conditions (Searle 1969) on appropriate indicating or demanding. It would appear that the child begins at this critical point to make a connection between his growing

lexical and syntactic competence and some early set of procedures for performing and interpreting performances of
illocutionary acts. Assuming the child sincerely wants such
utterances to be interpreted pragmatically as intended, it
follows that this new independence from explicit lexical
marking of utterance intent (as with the earlier *see* and *want*)
signals a tacit expectation on the child's part that his inter-
locutors are capable of inferring contextually the necessary
non-linguistic felicity conditions on at least some illocutionary
acts. This expectation will be rooted in the child's prior
sociocentric nature, as emphasised by Dr Bullowa, and will
be dependent upon many of the prelinguistically-acquired
skills she mentions for establishing and maintaining an intersubjective field.

A task I see as worth addressing by researchers is the
determination of the emergence point of competence for
one-many relations between an utterance's linguistic form
and its intended illocutionary force. For example, on a previous
occasion Professor Halliday pointed out that his subject Nigel
initially used forms like *more juice* exclusively as requests
or demands, while utterances of the form *two book* were
apparently never used to realise requests or demands (cited
in Ervin-Tripp 1974). Yet before long, we find young children
demonstrating adult-like capacity to distinguish performances
of a sentence like *would you like to do X?* uttered in an
appropriate *requesting* context from linguistically-identical
performances of the sentence uttered in an appropriate *yes-no
enquiry* context (Reeder 1975a, b). At some critical point, it
appears that children cut themselves adrift from the one form-
one function correspondence, and begin to employ what
Labov (1970) calls 'invariant rules of interpretation'. as
noted by Dr Widdowson. They move from competence for
'literal' or overtly-labelled speech acts to competence for
what Searle (1975) treats as 'indirect speech acts'. Now the
latter depend for their interpretation upon the use of propos-
itional-linguistic competence (Dr Widdowson's rules of usage)
together with some principles of co-operative conversation
(of the sort demonstrated in the studies reviewed above)
and an ability to draw inferences from context about participant
knowledge, intentions and attitudes. This latter skill I am

inclined to identify as a role-taking skill of the sort referred to earlier.

All these factors considered, I can only conclude that Gruber has pinpointed the convergence of some crucial, intersubjective aspects of communicative skills with ongoing syntactic and lexical development. It is as if parallel lines of development now intersect and create the conditions for the performance of non-literal, conveyed speech acts. I would contend that such indirect or conveyed speech acts constitute the normal state of affairs in mature language use, contrary to the impression given by some linguists and philosophers working in the area. As Labov (1970) demonstrates, sequencing rules in ordinary spontaneous conversation must be sensitive not to the overt syntactic form of each utterance in turn, but to the speech act being conveyed by each such turn in context. These speech acts in field data will seldom display their illocutionary forces in any overt linguistic way. At this point in the developmental schedule, it could be argued that adult-like rules for achieving coherent discourse become a part of the child's communicative competence.

Dr Bullowa is correct in observing that earliest communicative behaviour is about itself, concerned with the I-thou relation newly established and nurtured. But what Gruber's work on her data pinpoints, I think, is the inauguration of an apparently new, yet organically-emerging developmental period characterised by a powerful linking of these early speech acts, indicating and demanding, to already-developing inferential skills and interpersonal knowledge. Thus later communicative behaviour moves beyond itself to a point where it may better be regarded as interpersonal linguistic action.

II

It seems eminently useful for Dr Widdowson to have addressed here the question of what constitutes competence for discourse, and how this competence will be accounted for within a general theory of communicative competence. As has often been pointed out, it makes little sense attempting to chart the acquisition of something we know little about in its mature form. I shall begin my remarks on Dr Widdowson's presentation by querying his conceptions of the notion *rule*, and of the place of abstraction in theory-building, and conclude by responding to several of his observations, which seem to me rich with implications for current educational practice.

While Dr Widdowson correctly objects to a simplistic extension of rules hitherto regarded as appropriate in the domain of sentence grammar to the domain of connected discourse, that objection is directed toward something of a straw man. No discourse analysts I know of would see themselves working with a descriptive apparatus resembling the formation rules, say, of a Chomskyan transformational grammar. This is not to say that discourse analysis will not require tools of formalisation which permit statements of maximum generality and explicitness, that is, rules. Quite the contrary, still the best-known way in which to proceed from speculation about the organisational principles underlying appropriate, coherent discourse to provisional knowledge about these principles is by testing consequences of formal statements. Is Dr Widdowson suggesting that researchers, in dispensing with the notion of rule, abandon all attempts at theory construction and validation?

I suspect that Dr Widdowson would not regard as ill-conceived in principle at least one recent attempt to formalise conversational principles. Gordon and Lakoff (1971), for instance, formulate 'conversational postulates' to account for how utterances like *it's cold in here* may be interpreted conversationally in context as a request to shut the window. For all its inadequacies of detail, this remains a fruitful approach to theory-building at the level of illocutionary act competence and, I maintain, at the level of actual use of these acts. The interesting feature of conversational postulates is that such rules will not merely specify the set of assumptions which participants must share for a given illocutionary act (variants of Searle's contextual felicity conditions). In addition, the rule statement will specify in considerable detail the propositional content and syntactic form of utterances which may be used to perform that illocutionary act. Such rules will obviously bear little resemblance to grammatical rules, yet they represent an attempt to characterise the language user's knowledge of one of the formal systems of language, namely, how certain illocutionary acts may be conveyed and made sense of. Moreover, the inclusion of both linguistic and contextual constraints in these rules calls into question the need to distinguish 'rules of use' from 'procedures for use'. We return to this issue below.

If Dr Widdowson was objecting to the guise of precision under which many former approaches to rule-writing masqueraded, he might consider two current approaches that attempt to capture that variability he so correctly maintains must be taken into account sooner or later. Specifically, I think of Labov's concept of 'variable rule', which attempts to capture variability in applicability of certain syntactic and phonological processes, and of the generative semanticists' 'fuzzy rules', which attempt to take into account the fact that native speaker intuitions are not always as clear-cut as they might be in an ideal world. Formalisation neither necessarily implies simplistic accounts of only the clearest-cut phenomena, nor the sorts of 'absolute constraints' to which Dr Widdowson objects.

The suggestion that formalisation of rules of knowledge will necessarily fail to account for phenomena like metaphor is surely a red herring. The Prague School linguists point out, as has Chomsky in his earliest work, that much of our innovative behaviour will be accounted for in terms of exploitation of the very constraints captured by statements of general principles. Foregrounding presupposes the normative background.

Dr Widdowson discussed in some detail the well-known proposal by Labov (1970) to account for the way in which the utterance *well, when do you plan to come home*, for instance, may on some occasions of use be interpreted as a request that the hearer come home. Granted that Labov's formulation is partly inadequate, I believe it fails on grounds other than those to which Dr Widdowson objects.

What Labov's 'rule of interpretation' fails to do is capture an important generalisation about one class of necessary preconditions on appropriate requesting. Now Labov proposes that if A makes a request for information of B about whether an act X has been performed, and four additional assumptions Labov lists are shared by A and B, then A will be heard by B as making a request that B do act X. But a more general

statement of the linguistic preconditions, the constraints on
what a speaker can say in order to be heard as performing
such a request, includes Labov's example as a particular
case. Following Searle (1969) as to the necessary *propositional
content condition* on requesting, we need only require that A
predicate a future act **X**, and perhaps not even necessarily
predicate it of B in particular. In any case, I want to emphasise
that the speaker, A, need not perform one sort of illocutionary
act (requesting information of B) in order to convey another
(requesting that B do **X**). Rather, he need only utter a proposition meeting the minimum requirements just stated, in
a context meeting defined preconditions. Thus: *is the door
shut?, the door hasn't been shut, will you shut the door?,
when will you shut the door?, I want the door shut, I wonder
if you'd mind shutting the door, shut the door!,* and so on, can
all convey a request to B that B shut the door, when performed
in a requesting context. No request for information need
be performed; in fact, mere yes-no responses will be regarded
by A and B as clearly inappropriate responses to any of the
above interrogatives in co-operative conversation, where only
the guise of option-giving is operant in requesting contexts.
Syntactic mood for the input sentence will be assigned by
something like Labov's 'A-B events' principle, or better,
Forman's 'Speaker Knows Best' principle: say what you're
supposed to know about, and ask what you can't presume to
know. And to meet Widdowson's legitimate objection to Labov's
tactic of defining an interpretive rule for one illocutionary
act by employing a further act, itself undefined: 'say' and 'ask'
in Forman's principle must not be construed in illocutionary
terms, but in purely syntactic terms, in the sense of declarative
and interrogative mood, respectively. As has been pointed out,
no necessary connection between declarative syntax and acts
of asserting, or between interrogative syntax and acts of
enquiring can be demonstrated. (Who says we use interrogatives
only to ask questions?)

   In the light of this reformulation of Labov's *ad hoc* proposal
in the direction of Searle's more general approach to illocutionary act analysis, we find that the distinction disappears
between competence for speech acts (Dr Widdowson's rule
of use), in the sense of specifications of illocutionary acts'

necessary preconditions, and characterisations of procedures for using these acts. A sufficient characterisation of an illocutionary act will, as Searle makes clear, also contain some statement of necessary propositional content constraints upon utterances used to perform illocutionary acts. Labov simply missed this generalisation. Similarly, the 'conversational postulates' proposal of Gordon and Lakoff attempts a specification in more detail of possible propositional content for a few illocutionary acts, and seems in no way compatible with a rule-procedure distinction. Each postulate specifies in a single statement how to get from what is *said* propositionally to what is *done* pragmatically.

I am intrigued by Dr Widdowson's observation that rules of use will be subject to variation, the sense that an instance of the act 'agreement' in one domain need not constitute an instance thereof in a different domain. I would venture a guess that the same sort of variation might be expected across subcultural groups, and might account to a degree for instances of what we may term 'illocutionary interference'. Sinclair and Coulthard (1975) observe that in British Primary schools a teacher's question about why a pupil is doing something will ordinarily be taken as a proscription of whatever that pupil happened to be doing. Could some groups of pupils, by virtue of the interpretive rules to which they are accustomed in the community, find school learning more difficult because of the added burden of having to acquire a repertoire of classroom-specific interpretive procedures, many of which will not be reinforced in any other setting? More generally, the suggestion that educationalists view as a central task the extension and refinement of the illocutionary repertoire seems a rich basis for curriculum and instruction in a wide range of educational settings, but particularly for both first and second language instruction. Probably the best work to date along such lines has been in the field of English as a Second Language, done by those working within the framework of a communicatively or pragmatically-organised syllabus (Corder 1973: 317-20). See, for instance, the work of Dulay and Burt (1973), Paulston and Bruder (1976), Schumann (1972), and Widdowson (1972).

Dr Widdowson's observation that writing may be regarded as interactive is entirely correct, and not at all obvious, judging from a great deal of past pedagogical practice. Educationists who do recognise this fact are, however, beginning to mount proposals to exploit it in writing instruction. Britton, Martin and associates (1975) in a large-scale survey of British Primary and Secondary pupils' writing, discovered that a large proportion of writing done by Primary pupils could be regarded as having been consciously interactive in its genesis — what they termed 'expressive writing', something close to 'talk written down'. However, the Secondary pupils were producing writing which afforded very little evidence of this interactive characteristic of writing ever having been acknowledged, let alone employed in the instructional process. The latter sort of writing, dubbed 'transactional' by the researchers, accounted for almost all of the writing done at the top end of the Secondary sample. Two proposals serve as possible responses to Dr Widdowson's observation here. Moffett's (1968) scheme to encourage greater use of improvisational drama and role-play within the language classroom seems one appropriate avenue to explore. Current work in the U.S. in what are called 'real writing' programmes and approaches (Judy 1973) places a new emphasis upon the publication of the learner's written work before a wide range of possible audiences within school and community.

III

If a single theme were identified as having emerged from the present seminar, it would be the recognition of the deictic basis of competence for discourse. Professor Lyons argued for the deictic basis of anaphoric reference, appealing to the notions of third-order, intensional entities and salience within a universe of discourse. It is at that point that his remarks take on a rich significance for our understanding of discourse acquisition. Professor Halliday, in addition to having provided us with data bearing upon questions of discourse aquisition, introduced the concept of acquisition of generic structure as one of several aspects of the child's emerging ability to construct text or running discourse. In this concluding section, I shall register a few points of contact between these two discussions, some obvious enough, but a few less so.

Professor Halliday's claim that intuitions about discourse emerge even within the proto-language stage is based upon

striking prosodic evidence, and is particularly well-exemplified
in the 'naming game' routine, and the 'reparatory act' *dōubà*.
Where the early data bears upon emergence of intuitions about
conversational sequencing, later data on contrastive sentence
stress placement demonstrates that even very young children
have the capacity to formulate and use judgments about hearer
knowledge, even if inaccurately at times. One suspects that
some of the claims we reviewed earlier regarding communicative
egocentricity were formulated as much upon the basis of performance constraints on role-taking capacity as upon valid
measurement of the capacity itself. I would propose that in
addition to looking at Professor Lyons' 'textual deixis' for
evidence bearing upon the developmental mechanism underlying transition from deictic to anaphoric reference, we continue
to examine carefully the child's developing ability to establish
and maintain an intersubjective field. One thinks again of
the work of Dr Bullowa and associates in this respect, and of
Jerome Bruner and associates in the area of joint attention
(Scaife and Bruner 1975). Entailed by such ability would
seem to be a sub-skill for inferring a hearer's knowledge about,
and attitudes and intentions toward, a range of things, acts,
and states of affairs, or Professor Lyons' first and second-order
entities.

Professor Halliday's suggestion that early but-conjunction
seems not strictly anaphoric may be attributed to the fact
that a paraphrase of this sort of *but* would be 'contrary to
hearer's, and perhaps speaker's, expectations, S'. It is not
relations between clauses which are being encoded here, but
facts about expectations within speaker's and hearer's intersubjective field of discourse. The semantics of conjunction
will account for relations between intensional objects, propositions, held within the intersubjective field, not between linguistic realisations thereof. Now the psychologically-
functional counterpart of the transition from deictic to
anaphoric reference appears to be based initially at least upon
a capacity to manipulate objects and simple acts — first and
second-order entities — as described by the Piagetian account
of sensorimotor intelligence. The transition, however, seems
to involve the intensional counterparts of these first and
second-order entities, concepts and propositions, eventually

becoming potential objects of cognition and manipulation themselves.

One is struck by the resemblance between the manner in which Professor Lyons' third-order entities seem to operate within the intersubjective field of discourse, and recent accounts (Searle 1975, Reeder 1975b) of how contextual felicity conditions on illocutionary acts will be derived from shared knowledge and assumptions of participants, then employed in formulating and interpreting utterances as instances of particular illocutionary act types. It would appear that the phenomenon of reference is more closely bound up with contextual and pragmatic considerations than had been suspected.

Professor Halliday claims that one aspect of the child's emerging grasp of generic structure, narration, evolves from a 'mathetic' or 'declarative' act of meaning which is self-sufficient, and calls for no response. On the other hand, it was suggested that narrative is typically built up through conversation as an interactive process, as is illustrated by the way in which Nigel spins his tale of the goat. The postulation of a self-sufficient class or mode of meaning seems incompatible, first, with the success of recent discourse acquisition work based, like that of Bullowa, Garvey, Shatz, Keenan, and others, upon assumptions of initial sociocentricity. Second, recent linguistic accounts of declarative sentences (Ross 1970) and of the illocutionary act 'say' or 'assert' (Lakoff 1972) point to the interactive, response-expecting nature of such speech acts. Any parent who tries *not* to respond to a child's so-called 'simple active affirmative declarative' utterances soon learns what the child expects of a hearer in the way of conversational participation.

To return to Nigel's impressive narrative, Professor Halliday pointed out that Nigel at age 1;8 used a 'pragmatic' negative, but no 'mathetic' negative. In more conventional terms, Nigel's *no* and *shouldn't* were perhaps lexicalisations of an underlying performative predicate PROSCRIBE or, more probably, of the illocutionary act 'proscribe' or 'forbid', depending partly upon one's views about the performative analysis. Propositional negation, involving predication that some relation or state of affairs is not the case, has not been

lexicalised yet, but is being realised gesturally only. It seems
to me that Professor Lyons' useful distinction between second-
order entities (events, states of affairs, relations existing in
the physical world) and their third-order, intensional counterparts (concepts and propositions) may help explain the apparent
developmental gap between the two sorts of negation. Where
Nigel lexicalises a negative, it is an *act* within the situation,
a second-order entity, which is being proscribed. Deictic
reference (or predication) seems to account adequately for
such cases. Where negation is only gesturally realised, as in
(*not*) *good for it*, it is the truth value of a proposition within
the universe of discourse, a third-order entity, which is being
negated. It could be that at this stage, regardless of relative
salience of propositions within the universe of discourse, it
is a more complex task cognitively to negate a proposition
than it is to realise an (illocutionary) act with a negative
particle. Propositional negation is probably better regarded
as anaphoric predication, the deictic roots of anaphora not-
withstanding.

Does nature provide children with developmental cul-de-sacs?
At one point Professor Halliday observed that Nigel, in learning
how dialogue works, constructed models of that genre, which
seemed not to correspond to anything in the adult language.
Try as I may, I can find nothing in his data, nor can I imagine
acquisition strategies of any generality compatible with such
an observation. The recent history of language acquisition
studies bears out the theoretical utility of postulating organic
principles of development, rather than idiosyncratic, non-
continuous developmental stages. The demise of pivot grammar
is one rather obvious case (Bloom 1970, Brown 1973), and
recent work interpreting childen's semantic 'errors' in a
sophisticated manner is another (Donaldson and Wales 1970,
Clark 1973). If anything, Professor Halliday's data and developmental account of the growth of text-forming capacity seems
more in line with the very characteristics of organic growth
Dr Bullowa noted, progressive elaboration and differentiation
of skills. His work demonstrates the embryonic existence —
indeed within the proto-language — of elements shown independently to be necessary: semantic and pragmatic foundations
of mature communicative competence.

BIBLIOGRAPHY

Aaronson, D. and Rieber, W. (1975) (eds) *Developmental Psycholinguistics and Communication Disorders*. New York: New York Academy of Sciences

Abercrombie, D. (1967) *Elements of General Phonetics*. Edinburgh University Press

— (1968) Paralanguage. *British Journal of Disorders of Communication* 3, 55-9

Abramovici, S. and Myers, T.F. (1975) The semantic structure of spontaneous dialogue. Presented to the B.P.S. Conference on Language and the Social Context. Stirling, 10-11 January

Antinucci, F. (1974) Sulla deissi. Roma: Consiglio Nazionale delle Ricerche, Instituto di Psicologia. (Reported in Bates 1976)

Argyle, M. (1972) Non-verbal communication in human social interaction. In R.A. Hinde (ed) *Non-Verbal Communication*. Cambridge University Press

Atkinson, R.M. and Griffiths, P.D. (1973) Here's here's, there's, here and there. *Edinburgh Working Papers in Linguistics* 3, 29-73

Austin, J.L. (1962) *How to Do Things with Words*. Oxford University Press/Cambridge, Mass.: Harvard University Press

Barthes, R. (1970) *S/Z*. Paris: Seuil

Bates, E. (1976) *Language and Context: The Acquisition of Pragmatics*. New York, San Francisco and London: Academic Press

Bateson, G. (1955) A theory of play and fantasy; a report on theoretical aspects of the project for study of the role of paradoxes of abstraction in communication. Reprinted in G. Bateson (1972) *Steps to an Ecology of Mind*. Paladin

– (1966) Problems in cetacean and other mammalian communication. Reprinted in G. Bateson (1972) *Steps to an Ecology of Mind*. Paladin

– (1972) The logical categories of learning and communication. In G. Bateson: *Steps to an Ecology of Mind*. Paladin

Bateson, M.C. (1971) The interpersonal context of infant vocalization. Quarterly Progress Report of the Research Laboratory of Electronics, M.I.T., 100, 170-76

– (1975) Mother-infant exchanges: the epigenesis of conversational interaction. In Aaronson and Rieber (1975)

Benveniste, E. (1956) La nature des pronoms. In *For Roman Jakobson*. The Hague: Mouton. Reprinted in *Problèmes de Linguistique Générale*. Paris: Gallimard 1966

Bloom, L. (1970) Why not pivot grammar? *Journal of Speech and Hearing Disorders* 36, 40-50

– (1973) *One Word at a Time*. The Hague: Mouton

Bower, T.G.R. (1972) Object perception in infants. *Perception* 1, 15-20

Britton, J. et al. (1975) *The Development of Writing Abilities*. London: Macmillan

Brown, R. (1973) *A First Language: The Early Stages*. London: George Allen and Unwin

Bruner, J.S. (1975) From communication to language – a psychological perspective. *Cognition* 3(3), 255-87

– (1976) On prelinguistic prerequisites of speech. Presented at the NATO Conference on the Psychology of Language, Stirling. June

Bühler, K. (1934) *Sprachtheorie*. Jena: Fischer (Reprinted, Stuttgart: Fischer 1965)

Bullowa, M., Jones, L.G. and Bever, T.G. (1964) Development from vocal to verbal behaviour in children. Monographs of the Society for Research in Child Language 29(1), 101-7

Butterworth, B. and Beattie, G. (1976) Gesture and silence as indicators of planning in speech. Presented at the NATO Conference on the Psychology of Language, Stirling. June

Carnap, R. (1956) *Meaning and Necessity*, 2nd ed. Chicago University Press

Chomsky, N. (1957) *Syntactic Structures*. The Hague: Mouton
— (1969) Deep structure, surface structure and semantic interpretation. In D.D. Steinberg & L.A. Jakobovits (eds) *Semantics*. London and New York: Cambridge University Press

Clark, E. (1973) What's in a word? On the child's acquisition of semantics in his first language. In T. Moore (ed) *Cognitive Development and Acquisition of Language*. New York and London: Academic Press

Clarke, D. (1975) The use and recognition of sequential structure in dialogue. *British Journal of Social and Clinical Psychology* 14 (4), 333-9

Collis, G.M. and Schaffer, H.R. (1975) Synchronization of visual attention in mother-infant pairs. *Journal of Child Psychology and Psychiatry*

Condon, W.S. and Sander, L.W. (1974) Neonate movement is synchronized with adult speech: interactional participation and language acquisition. *Science* 183, 99-101

Corder, S.P. (1973) *Introducing Applied Linguistics*. Harmondsworth: Penguin

Crymes, R. (1968) *Some Systems of Substitution Correlations in Modern American English*. The Hague: Mouton

Crystal, D. (1975) *The English Tone of Voice*. London: Edward Arnold

Culler, J. (1975) *Structuralist Poetics*. London: Routledge & Kegan Paul

Daneš, F. (ed) (1974) *Papers on Functional Sentence Perspective*. Prague: Academia (Czechoslovak Academy of Sciences)

De Laguna, G. (1927) *Speech: Its Function and Development*. Bloomington: Indiana University Press

Denzin, N.K. (1972) Childhood as a conversation of gestures. *Sociol. Symp.* 7

Donaldson, M. and Wales, R.J. (1970) On the acquisition of some relational terms. In Hayes, J.R. (ed) *Cognition and the Development of Language*. New York: Wiley

Dore, J. (1974) A pragmatic description of early language development. *Journal of Psycholinguistic Research* 3, 343-50

— (1975) Holophrases, speech acts and language universals. *Journal of Child Language* 2, 21-40

— (1977) Children's illocutionary acts. In R.O. Freedle (ed) *Discourse Production and Comprehension*. Hillsdale, New Jersey: Lawrence Erlbaum Associates

Ducrot, O. and Todorov, T. (1972) *Dictionnaire Encyclopedique des Sciences du Langage*. Paris: Seuil

Dulay, H. and Burt, M. (1973) Should we teach children syntax? *Language Learning* 23, 245-58

Duncan, S.D. Jr. (1972) Some signals and rules for taking speaking turns in conversation. *Journal of Personality and Social Psychology* 23, 283-92

— (1973) Towards a grammer for dyadic conversation. *Semiotica* 9, 29-46

— (1975) Interaction units during speaking turns in dyadic, face-to-face conversation. In A. Kendon, R.M. Harris and M.R. Key (eds) *Organization of Behaviour in Face-to-Face Interaction*. The Hague: Mouton

Eibl-Eibesfeldt, I. (1972) Similarities and differences between cultures in expressive movements. In R.A. Hinde (ed) *Non-Verbal Communication*. Cambridge University Press

Eisenberg, R.B. (1975) Auditory sensory processes: some gleanings from the developmental lode. In Prescott, Read and Coursin (eds) *Brain Function and Malnutrition: Neurological Methods of Assessment*. New York: Wiley

Ekman, P., and Friesen, W.V. (1969) The repertoire of non-verbal behaviour: categories, origins, usage and coding. *Semiotica* 1, 49-98

Erickson, F. (1975) One function of proxemic shifts in face-to-face interaction. In A. Kendon, R.M. Harris and M.R. Key (eds) *Organization of Behaviour in Face-to-Face Interaction*. The Hague: Mouton

Ervin-Tripp, S. (1974) The comprehension and production of requests by children. Papers and Reports on Child Language Development (Stanford University) 8, 188-96

Ferguson, N. (1976) Interruptions: speaker-switch nonfluency in spontaneous conversation. In A. Kemp, E. Uldall and J. Miller (eds) *Work in Progress, No. 9*. Department of Linguistics, Edinburgh University

Fillenbaum, S. (1976) How to do some things with IF. Presented at the NATO Conference on the Psychology of Language, Stirling. June

Fillmore, C.J. (1971) Verbs of judging: an exercise in semantic description. In C.J. Fillmore and D.T. Langendoen (eds) *Studies in Linguistic Semantics*. New York: Holt, Rinehart and Winston

Flavell, J.H. et al. (1968) *The Development of Role-taking and Communication Skills in Children*. New York: Wiley

Forman, D. (1974) The speaker knows best principle. In *Papers from the Tenth Regional Meeting of the Chicago Linguistic Society*, Chicago Linguistic Society 162-77

France, M.N. (1975) *The Generation of the Self: A Study of the Construction of Categories in Infancy*. Ph.D. Thesis, University of Essex

Garvey, C. and Hogan, R. (1973) Social speech and social interaction: egocentrism revisited. *Child Development* 44, 562-8

Gelman, R. and Shatz, M. (1977) Appropriate speech adjustments: the operation of conversational constraints on talk to two-year-olds. In M. Lewis, and L. Rosenblum (eds) *Interaction, Conversation, and the Development of Language*. New York: Wiley

Gesell, A., Ilg, F.L. and Bullis, G.E. (1949) *Vision: Its Development in Infant and Child*. New York: Paul B. Hoeber

Goffman, E. (1974) *Frame Analysis*. New York: Harper & Row

Gordon, D. and Lakoff, G. (1971) Conversational Postulates. In *Papers from the Seventh Regional Meeting of the Chicago Linguistic Society*, 63-84. Chicago: Chicago Linguistic Society

Grice, H.P. (1957) Meaning. *Philosophical Review,* 377-88
– (1975) Logic and conversation. In P. Cole and J.L. Morgan (eds) *Syntax and Semantics: Volume 3: Speech Acts*. London, San Francisco and New York: Academic Press

Gruber, J.S. (1973) Correlations between the syntactic constructions of the child and of the adult. In C.A. Ferguson and D. Slobin (eds) *Studies of Child Language*. New York: Holt, Rinehart and Winston

— (1975) Performative-constative transition in child language. *Foundations of Language* 12, 513-27

Gunter, J. (1972) Intonation and Relevance. In D.L. Bolinger (ed) *Intonation*. Harmondsworth: Penguin

Halliday, M.A.K. (1967/8) Notes on transitivity and theme in English. *Journal of Linguistics* 3, 37-81; 199-244 and *J. Ling.* 4, 179-215

— (1970a) Language structure and language function. In J. Lyons (ed) *New Horizons in Linguistics*. Harmondsworth: Penguin

— (1970b) *A Course in Spoken English*. London: Oxford University Press

— (1973) *Explorations in the Functions of Language*. London: Edward Arnold

— (1975) *Learning How to Mean: Explorations in the Development of Language*. London: Edward Arnold

Halliday, M.A.K. and Hasan, R. (1976) *Cohesion in English*. London: Longmans (English Language Series 9)

Hasan, R. (1968) *Grammatical Cohesion in Spoken and Written English Pt 1*. London: Longmans

Hinde, R.A. (1974) *Biological Bases of Human Social Behaviour*. London and New York: McGraw-Hill Book Co.

Hjelmslev, L. (1937) La nature du pronom. In *Mélanges . . . Jacques van Gimmeken*. Paris: Klincksieck

Huxley, R. (1970) The development of the correct use of subject personal pronouns in two children. In G.B. Flores d'Arcais and W.J.M. Levelt (eds) *Advances in Psycholinguistics*. Amsterdam: North Holland

Isard, S. (1975a) Changing the context. In E.L. Keenan (ed) *Formal Semantics of Natural Language*. London, New York and Melbourne: Cambridge University Press

— (1975b) On getting things into context. In E.L. Keenan (ed) *Formal Semantics of Natural Language*. London and New York: Cambridge University Press

Jackendoff, R.S. (1972) *Semantic Interpretation in Generative Grammar*. Cambridge, Mass.: M.I.T. Press

Jaffe, J., Stern, D.N. and Peery, J.C. (1973) 'Conversational' coupling of gaze behaviour in prelinguistic human development. *Journal of Psycholinguistic Research* 2 (4), 321-9

Jespersen, O. (1946) *A Modern English Grammar, Volume 4*. London: Allen & Unwin

Judy, S.N. (1973) Writing for the here and now. *English Journal* 62, 69-79

Katz, J. (1972) *Semantic Theory*. New York: Harper & Row

Keenan, E.O. (1974) Conversational competence in children. *Journal of Child Language* 1, 163-83

— (1975) Again and again: the pragmatics of repetition in child language. *Pragmatics Microfiche* 1, 5

Kendon, A. (1967) Some functions of gaze direction in social interaction. *Acta Psychologica* 26, 22-63

— (1973) The role of visible behaviour in the organization of social interaction. In M. von Cranach and I. Vine (eds) *Social Communication and Movement: Studies of Interaction and Expression in Man and Chimpanzee*. London and New York: Academic Press

— (1976) Gesticulation, speech and the gesture theory of language origins. In S.K. Ghosh (ed) *Biology and Language*. Baltimore: University Park Press

Key, M.R. (1970) Preliminary remarks on paralanguage and kinesics in human communication. *La Linguistique* 6(2), 17-36

Klaus, M. et al. (1970) Human maternal behaviour at the first contact with her young. *Pediatrics* 46

Klima, E.S. and Bellugi, U. (1975) Perception and production in a visually based language. In Aaronson and Rieber (1975)

Kristeva, J. (1969) *Semeiotike*. Paris: Seuil

Labov, W. (1969) The logic of non-standard English. Reprinted in P.P. Giglioni (ed) *Language and Social Context*. Penguin Modern Psychology Readings

— (1970) The study of language in its social context. *Studium Generale* 23, 66-84

— (1972) *Sociolinguistic Patterns*. Philadelphia: University of Pennsylvania Press

Lakoff, R. (1972) Language in context. *Language* 48, 907-27

— (1974) Remarks on *this* and *that*. In *Berkeley Studies in Syntax and Semantics*, Vol. 1. University of California, Berkeley: Department of Linguistics

Laver, J. and Hutcheson, S. (1972) (eds) *Communication in Face-to-Face Interaction*. Harmondsworth: Penguin

Lomax, A. (1975) Culture-style factors in face-to-face interaction. In A. Kendon, R.M. Harris & M.R. Key (eds) *Organization of Behaviour in Face-to-Face Interaction*. Mouton

Lyons, J. (1968) *Introduction to Theoretical Linguistics*. Cambridge University Press

— (1972) Human language. In R.A. Hinde (ed) *Non-Verbal Communication*. Cambridge University Press

— (1975) Deixis as the source of reference. In E.L. Keenan (ed) *Formal Semantics of Natural Languages*. London and New York: Cambridge University Press

— (1977) *Semantics, Vols. 1 and 2*. London and New York: Cambridge University Press

Lyons, J., Atkinson, R.M., Griffiths, P.D. and Macrae, A. (1975) The Linguistic Development of Young Children. Final Report to the Social Sciences Research Council

MacKay, D.M. (1972) Formal analysis of communicative processes. In R.A. Hinde (ed) *Non-Verbal Communication* Cambridge University Press

Malinowski, B. (1923) The problem of meaning in primitive languages. Supplement to C.K. Ogden and I.A. Richards (eds) *The Meaning of Meaning*, 8th edition. London: Routledge & Kegan Paul, 1946 (First edition, 1923)

Markel, N.N. (1975) Coverbal behaviour associated with conversation turns. In A. Kendon, R.M. Harris & M.R. Key (eds) *Organization of Behaviour in Face-to-Face Interaction*. Mouton

Masangky, Z.S. et al. (1974) The early development of inferences about the visual percepts of others. *Child Development* 45, 357-66

Menzel, E.W. (1971) Communication about the environment in a group of young chimpanzees. *Folia Primatologia* 15, 220-32

— (1975) Natural language of young chimpanzees. *New Scientist*, 16 January

Miller, G.A. and Johnson-Laird, P.N. (1976) *Language and Perception*. Cambridge, Mass.: The Belknap Press of Harvard University Press

Moffett, J. (1968) *Teaching the Universe of Discourse*. Boston: Houghton-Mifflin

Myers, T.F. (1975) The onset of dialogue. Presented to the Third International Child Language Conference. London

Nelson, K. (1973) Structure and strategy in learning to talk. Monographs of the Society for Research in Child Development, 38 (nos. 1-2, serial no. 149)

Paulston, C.B. and Bruder, M.N. (1976) *Teaching English as a Second Language: Techniques and Procedures*. Cambridge, Mass.: Winthrop

Peirce, C. (1932) *Collected Papers*. C. Hartshorne and P. Weiss (eds). Cambridge, Mass.: Harvard University Press

Piaget, J. (1926) *Language and Thought of the Child*. New York: Harcourt Brace

— (1970) Piaget's theory. In P. Mussen (ed) *Carmichael's Manual of Child Psychology*. New York: Wiley

Reeder, K.F. (1975a) On young children's discrimination of illocutionary force. *Pragmatics Microfiche* 1, 5

— (1975b) *Pre-school Children's Comprehension of Illocutionary Force: An Experimental Psycholinguistic Study*. Doctoral thesis, University of Birmingham

Ross, J.R. (1970) On declarative sentences. In R.A. Jacobs and P.S. Rosenbaum (eds) *Readings in English Transformational Grammar*. Waltham, Mass.: Ginn

Sacks, R. (1972) On the analyzability of stories by children. In J.J. Gumperz and D. Hymes (eds) *Directions in Sociolinguistics: the Ethnography of Communication.* New York: Holt, Rinehart and Winston

Sacks, H., Schegloff, E.A. and Jefferson, G. (1974) A simplest systematics for the organization of turn-taking in conversation. *Language* 50, 696-735

Sadock, J.M. (1972) Speech Act Idioms. In *Papers from the Eighth Regional Meeting of the Chicago Linguistic Society.* Chicago: Chicago Linguistic Society

– (1975) *Toward a Linguistic Theory of Speech Acts.* New York: Academic Press

Sag, I.A. and Liberman, M. (1975) The intonational disambiguation of indirect speech acts. In *Papers from the Eleventh Regional Meeting of the Chicago Linguistic Society.* Chicago: Chicago Linguistic Society

Scaife, M. and Bruner, J. (1975) The capacity for joint visual attention in the infant. *Nature* 253, 265-6

Scheflen, A.E. (1972) *Body language and the social order.* Englewood Cliffs, New Jersey: Prentice-Hall

– (1975) Models and epistemologies in the study of interaction. In A. Kendon, R.M. Harris and M.R. Key (eds) *Organization of Behaviour in Face-to-Face Interaction.* The Hague and Paris: Mouton

Schegloff, E.A. and Sacks, H. (1973) Opening up closings. *Semiotica* 8, 289-327

Schmerling, S.F. (1976) *Aspects of English Sentence Stress.* University of Texas Press

Schumann, J. (1972) Communication techniques. *TESOL Quarterly* 6, 143-61

Searle, J.R. (1969) *Speech Acts: An Essay in the Philosophy of Language.* Cambridge University Press

– (1975) Indirect Speech Acts. In P. Cole and J.L. Morgan (eds) *Syntax and Semantics, Volume 3: Speech Acts.* London, San Francisco and New York: Academic Press

– (1976) A classification of speech acts. *Language and Society* 5, 1-23

Shatz, M. and Gelman, R. (1973) The development of communication skills: modifications in the speech of young children as a function of listener. Monographs of the Society for Research in Child Development 38, 1-37

Shepherd, H. (1976) *A Further Investigation of Non-Fluent Speaker-Switches*. Undergraduate Thesis in Psychology, University of Edinburgh

Sinclair, J.M. and Coulthard, M. (1975) *Towards the Analysis of Discourse*. London: Oxford University Press

Starr, S. (1975) The relationship of single words to two-word sentences. *Child Development* 46, 701-8

Stern, D.N. (1971) A micro-analysis of mother-infant interaction: behaviour regulating social contact between a mother and her 3½ months old twins. *Journal of the American Academy of Child Psychiatry* 10(3), 501-17

Stern, D.N. et al. (1975) Vocalizing in unison and in alternation: two modes of communication within the mother-infant dyad. In Aaronson and Rieber (1975)

Strawson, P.F. (1975) *Subject and Predicate*. London: Methuen

Vygotsky, L.S. (1962) *Thought and Language*. Cambridge, Mass.: M.I.T. Press

Waterson, N. and Snow, C. (1977) (eds) *The Development of Communication: Social and Pragmatic Factors in Language Acquisition*. London: John Wiley

Werner, H. and Kaplan, B. (1963) *Symbol Formation: An Organismic Developmental Approach to Language and the Expression of Thought*. John Wiley

Widdowson, H.G. (1972) The teaching of English as communication. *English Language Teaching* 27, 15-19

— (1973) *An Applied Linguistic Approach to Discourse Analysis*. Ph.D. Thesis, University of Edinburgh